Exploring Creation

with

Botany

by Jeannie K. Fulbright

Exploring Creation With Botany

Published by
Apologia Educational Ministries, Inc.
1106 Meridian Plaza, Suite 220
Anderson, IN 46016
www.apologia.com

Manufactured in the United States of America
Fourth Printing 2007

ISBN: 1-932012-49-4

Printed by CJK, Cincinnati, OH

Cover photos from www.clipart.com and copyright © Photodisc, Inc.   Cover design by Kim Williams

Need Help?

Apologia Educational Ministries, Inc. Curriculum Support

If you have any questions while using Apologia curriculum,
feel free to contact us in any of the following ways:

By Mail: Curriculum Help
Apologia Educational Ministries, Inc.
1106 Meridian Plaza, Suite 220
Anderson, IN 46016

By E-MAIL: help@apologia.com

On The Web: http://www.apologia.com

By FAX: (765) 608 - 3290

By Phone: (765) 608 - 3280

*Illustrations from the MasterClips
collection and the Microsoft Clip Art
Gallery*

Scientific Speculation Sheet

Name _____ **Date** _____

Experiment Title _____

Materials Used:

Procedure: (What you will do or what you did)

Hypothesis: (What you think will happen and why)

Results: (What actually happened)

Conclusion: (What you learned)

Introduction

Congratulations on your choice of *Exploring Creation with Botany* as your science course this year. You will find this to be an easy-to-use science program for elementary students. The book is written directly to the student, making it appealing to kids. Presenting science concepts in a conversational, engaging style makes science enchanting and memorable for your students. It also fosters a love for learning. This course is written for children between six and twelve years old. When the course is complete, this book will serve as an excellent reference for your family's future questions and studies in botany. As a result, this book is a life-long investment!

The Immersion Approach
"Is it Okay to Spend a Year on Botany?"

Many educators promote the spiral approach to education. In this approach, a student is exposed over and over again to minute amounts of a variety of science topics. The theory goes that we just want to 'expose' the student to science at this age, each year giving a bit more information than was given the year before. This method has proven unsuccessful in public and private schools. It assumes the young child is unable to understand profound scientific truths. If a child is presented scant and insufficient science, she will fail to develop a love for the subject, because it seems rather uninteresting. If the learning is skimpy, the subject seems monotonous. The student is simply scratching the surface of the amazing and fascinating information available in science. Sadly, students taught in this way are led to believe they "know all about" that subject, when in reality the subject is so much richer than they were allowed to know or explore. That is why we recommend that kids, even young kids, are given an in-depth exposure into each science topic. You, the educator, have the opportunity to abandon methods that don't work so that your students can learn in ways that are more effective. The immersion approach is the way everyone, even young kids, learn best. That is why we major in one field in college and take many classes in that field alone. If you immerse your student in one field of science for an entire year, he will develop a love for both that subject and a love for learning in general.

On the other hand, if a student rushed through several fields of science in one year, she will feel insecure about the information. In fact, she probably doesn't really know much science, and that's why she feels insecure. Imagine the benefit to your student when she is able to authentically converse with a scientist at a botanical garden, intelligently discussing the details of plant reproduction or the lifecycle of a fern. This will delight both your student and adults with conversation that is actually interesting and intelligent. A child taught with the immersion approach learns to love knowledge and develop confidence.

Additionally, a child that is focused on one subject throughout an entire year is being challenged mentally in ways that will develop his ability to think critically and retain complex information. This will actually benefit the student and give him an advantage on achievement tests. He will be able to make more intelligent inferences about the right answer on a science question, as God has created an orderly world that works very similarly throughout all subjects of science. A child who has not been given the deeper, more profound information will not understand how the scientific world operates, and he will not be able to reason through the problem to get the correct answer.

Lesson Increments

The lessons in this book are in-depth, some are lengthy, and they all contain quite a bit of scientific information. Each lesson should be broken up into manageable time slots depending on child's age and attention span. This will vary from family to family. There are 13 lessons in this text. Most lessons can be divided into two week segments; reading the text and doing the notebook assignments the first week, and working on the projects with data recording the second week. If you do science two or three days per week, you can read four to seven pages a day to finish a lesson and begin the project. Three of the lessons (1,4, and 6) are quite a bit longer than the average. They will probably require three weeks of study each. However, four of the lessons (8, 11-13) are shorter than the average, so they will each probably take less than two weeks to complete. This will give you 27-30 weeks for the entire book, allowing for leniency with vacations and family emergencies or lessons and experiments that might take a little longer than expected.

There are no workbooks or tests that go with this program, as I think this is unnecessary at this age. Instead, the very effective method of narrating and keeping notebooks is used. This is a superior method of facilitating retention and providing documentation of your child's education.

Narrations

Older elementary students can do the entire book and most of the experiments on their own, while younger students will enjoy an older sibling or parent reading it to them. Each lesson begins with reading the text. Throughout the reading, the student will be asked to retell or narrate the information she just studied. This helps the student to assimilate the information in her mind. The act of verbalizing it in her own words propels her forward in her ability to effectively and clearly communicate the information to others. It also serves to lock the information into her mind.

Please don't skip the narrations. Though they may seem to take up valuable time, they are vital to your students' intellectual development. The more narrating the student does, the better at it he will

become. The better the student becomes at narrating, the better he will be at writing, researching, and clearly communicating his beliefs. Some teachers encourage their students to take notes as they listen to reading. You may or may not want to try this.

The narration prompts are usually found under the title "What Do You Remember." Sometimes, however, there are narration prompts that are centered and in italics. Those prompts specifically tell the student to explain what he has learned to someone else. At the end of the day's reading, your student should write down or dictate to you what she remembers from the lesson. This written narration will be put in her notebook. At that time, you will have your student make an illustration to accompany her written narrative. If the student habitually restates her learning, adding these accounts to her botany notebook, she will accrue a volume of her own work that can be referred to repeatedly throughout the year.

Answers to the Narrative Questions

Near the back of the book, you will find a section named "Answers to the Narrative Questions." If you do not know an answer to one of the narrative questions, you should look at this section. This section also contains the expected results of certain experiments.

Notebooks

In addition to the written narrative, notebook activities promote further experience with the material. These activities are often entertaining and sometimes challenging to the students. Each notebook activity requires the student to utilize the material he learned in a creative way that will further enhance his retention. The notebook activities generally occur at the end of a lesson. It is recommended that you also include a narrative of any related field trips, projects, or activities.

Encourage your student to treasure his notebook, seeking to do his best work. His notebook is an important tool which will provide you and your student with a record of his course work. It will also serve as a foundation for future studies when the student is ready to take learning to the next level. Your student's notebook will spark lifelong memories of his homeschooling experience. Require diligence regarding his notebook.

Demonstrations and Projects

Most of the lessons contain hands-on demonstrations, which help bring the concept to your child's level of comprehension. There are also foundational projects in every lesson that will occasionally take a couple of weeks to complete. Though they may seem time consuming, these demonstrations and experiments are important to the subject and will benefit your child immensely. Please try very hard not to skip these demonstrations and projects. Your child should familiarize himself with the scientific method of hypothesizing and recording results, as that is required in the upper-level sciences. A **Scientific Speculation Sheet** is provided on page iv for your child to copy into her notebook. If you prefer, you have permission to make photocopies of that page.

In some of the projects and activities in the course, the student is asked to predict what will happen. Because of this, the expected results of the experiment are not given. If you are unsure about what should happen in the experiment, you should check the "Answers to the Narrative Questions" section near the back of the book. In addition to narrative question answers, this section contains the expected outcomes of such experiments.

Term Projects

There are two term projects your child will be asked to complete. The first is in Lesson 1 and the second is in Lesson 6. The first entails building a light hut that will be used to germinate seedlings indoors during any season of the year. It uses a florescent light that can be left on throughout the germination process, as it uses very little energy. The child is encouraged to use his light hut in many projects throughout the course.

The second term project will require your child to create her own field guide of the flora in her yard or neighborhood. It is a great idea to familiarize your child with the formatting of different field guides. She can make this field guide as thorough and complete as she wishes. Some children love to make books, and some will not find it as enjoyable. In either case, children will gain valuable insight into the plant life in their area as they attempt to research, document, illustrate, and categorize the plants they find.

The projects and experiments in this book use common, household items. As a result, they are fairly inexpensive, but you will have to hunt down everything that you need. To aid you in this, pages x and xi contain a list of the materials that you need for the activities and projects in each lesson. If you would rather spend some money for the sake of convenience, you can purchase a kit that goes with this course. It is sold through a company called "Creation Sensation," and you can contact them at 501-776-3147. Alternately, you can visit their website at http://www.creationsensation.com/.

Latin Root Words

There are a great many Latin words in science. Latin is the foundation of many languages, and knowing Latin roots aids a student extensively in understanding our language. This book will often define the Latin terms, breaking the word down into its root forms. It would benefit your student to take notes when she reads and copy all the Latin roots she learns into a separate Latin notebook. This notebook will serve the student well throughout her academic years, as it will provide the groundwork for later language study.

Course Website

If your child would like to learn more botany than what is contained in this course, there is a course website that allows the student to learn more about the wonderful world of plants. To go to the course website, simply type the following address into your web browser:

http://www.apologia.com/bookextras

You will see a box on the page. Type the following password into the box:

Godmadeflowers

Make sure you capitalize the first letter, and make sure there are no spaces in the password. When you hit "enter," you will be taken to the course website.

Items Needed To Complete Each Lesson

Every child will need his own notebook, blank paper, lined paper, and colored pencils.

Lesson 1

- A large assortment of shoes
- Leaf from a plant
- Paper towel
- Water (used in many lessons)
- An empty "copy paper" box, or shipping box
- Aluminum foil (approximately 10-15 feet)
- Electrical cord
- A light socket with plug
- Plastic plate or lid (such as the lid to an oatmeal, large yogurt, or sour cream container)
- Glue (used in many lessons)
- Scissors (used in many lessons)
- A 15-watt fluorescent spiral light (Most stores such as Wal-Mart carry these lights.)
- Peat moss
- Seeds for the plants you have decided to grow
- Containers for your plants (Styrofoam cups will work, but small plant pots are ideal.)
- Saucers or plastic lids
- Small paper bags
- String
- Glycerin soap bars for soap making (You can order these from any soap-making supplies store.)
- Glass measuring cup or bowl
- Soap mold (A disposable plastic container works great, but fancy molds are available for a few dollars at any craft store.)
- Olive oil or Vaseline®
- Dried herbs that you grew, and any other additives such as *Aloe vera*, vitamin E, cold-pressed olive oil, or ground oatmeal
- Craft sticks for stirring
- Fragrance: essential oils or fragrance oils found at health food stores
- Microwave or double boiler

Lesson 2

- A magnifying glass (used in many lessons)
- Sunflower seed
- Several bean seeds
- A pad of paper (You can staple pieces of paper together to make one if you don't have one.)
- Three plastic Ziploc® bags
- Three paper towels
- Three or more turnip seeds (or bean seeds)
- Tape (used in many lessons)
- A ruler (It should read centimeters.)

Lesson 3

- A flower (This cannot be a composite flower. It must have visible stamens and a carpel, such as the flower pictured on page 39.)
- A piece of paper
- An adult with a knife
- Construction paper (a bright color)
- Play-Doh®, clay, or salt dough (1 cup of flour, ¼ cup salt, ¼- ½ cup water)
- Cotton swabs (such as Q-tips®) or pipe cleaners
- A fresh flower
- A box that can close
- Borax

Lesson 4

- Two flowers that are still on their plants. (They should be on two separate plants of the same type. If you have a squash plant, you only need one flower.)
- A cotton swab (like a Q-tip®)
- Seeds for plants that butterflies like to eat and lay eggs on (See pp. 69-70 for plants that will work for butterflies in your area.)

Lesson 5

♦ Burr
♦ A file folder to serve as the game board
♦ Index cards
♦ Colored pencils
♦ Different nuts or pods to use as game pieces (peanut, walnut, pecan, acorn, for example)
♦ A six-sided die
♦ A squash or medium-sized pumpkin
♦ An adult with a sharp knife
♦ A dandelion tuft
♦ A samara
♦ A piece of paper
♦ A measuring device such as measuring tape or a ruler

Lesson 6

♦ Two plants (any kind)
♦ A plastic sandwich bag
♦ A clothespin
♦ A living plant that is not an evergreen
♦ Field guides that identify plants in your area
♦ An adult
♦ A leaf or leaves
♦ A stove
♦ A pot for boiling
♦ 3 tablespoons of washing soda (You can find this in the laundry section of the grocery store.)
♦ Gloves
♦ A spatula
♦ Paper towels

Lesson 7

♦ 2 carrots
♦ A knife
♦ 1 cup of water
♦ Blue food coloring
♦ A bulb from a plant (The best bulbs to force are paper white narcissus and hyacinths. Other bulbs will work, but do some research, because not all bulbs force easily.)
♦ A pot of soil
♦ A thermometer that reads in the 40º to 60º F range

Lesson 8

♦ A stalk of celery with the leaves still on it
♦ Cup
♦ Food coloring (red or blue)
♦ Clay or Play-Doh®
♦ Two paper or Styrofoam® cups with lids (You should not be able to see light through them.)
♦ Two bean seeds
♦ Two peat pellets for germinating seeds
♦ A sharpened pencil
♦ Black paint or black permanent marker
♦ Black paper

Lesson 9

♦ A 12-inch ruler
♦ Someone to help you
♦ Measuring tape or yardstick

♦ A tall tree
♦ Field guide that identifies trees (Suggestions are given on p. 134.)
♦ A crayon with all the paper removed
♦ Plain white paper
♦ Tacks (optional)

Lesson 10

♦ Two plastic sandwich bags
♦ Two clothespins
♦ Pinecone
♦ Oven preheated to 250 degrees
♦ Bucket of cold water

Lesson 11

♦ Paper
♦ Several fern fronds
♦ Several colors of paint
♦ A paint brush or sponge
♦ A fern frond with sori
♦ A paper towel
♦ A hardcover book

Lesson 12

♦ A coat hanger
♦ Yarn
♦ Trees with lichen on them, preferably in different places

Lesson 13
♦ A cereal box
♦ Yarn or ribbon
♦ A hole puncher
♦ Fabric or construction paper for the cover

Exploring Creation With Botany
Table of Contents

Lesson 1
Botany

Have you ever heard the word **botany** (bot' uh nee)? I didn't hear that word until I became an adult. Botany is the study of plants. It's an amazing field of science, and I know you will enjoy learning about it. You see, botany will tell you a lot about nature. After all, when you go outside to play, what do you see all around you? You see plants. The grass and trees that grow in the park are plants. The pretty flowers you see in the spring and summer are produced by plants. When you learn botany, you learn a lot about these plants, and it helps you understand what you see when you are out in nature.

In this course, you will learn a lot about plants, and you will do many experiments to help you understand how God designed them. Each day, when you are done with the reading, you will write down all that you remember about what you learned. This means you need to pay close attention so that you can remember what you are learning. Scientists often make illustrations (drawings) that go along with their notes. Since this is a science course, you will often make illustrations when you write down what you have learned.

Botany is the study of plants. This boy is doing botany, because he is studying a plant with a magnifying glass.

Look at the boy in the picture shown above. He has a small magnifying glass and is very carefully studying a flower. That means he is doing botany! Learning about plants will make studying even the smallest ones very interesting. Once you have studied about flowers, you may want to do what this boy is doing and carefully study the flowers that pop up in your yard or neighborhood. As you take this course, you will come to understand a lot about the plants you see all around you. If you pay close attention while reading this book, you'll even be able to teach others about botany!

How many different kinds of plants do you have around your home? Are there many trees in your neighborhood? Trees are big, tall plants. Do you have a pond or a creek near your home? If so, you probably have plants like mosses and ferns growing around it. Is there grass outside? Grass is a plant that covers the dirt like a rug. As you can see, there are plants all around you.

In Genesis 1:11-13, we learn that God created plants on the third day of creation. The plants He created are very interesting. They all make their own food; some trap insects inside of them; and some can grow taller than a skyscraper. The oldest living thing we know of on earth is a plant; it began growing right after the worldwide Flood and is still growing today! You will learn about many of these plants in this course, and you will see that God really used a *lot* of creativity when designing the plant world.

A magnifying glass helps us see things better by making them look bigger.

The plants of the world truly magnify the Lord. Are you wondering what it means to "magnify" the Lord? Well, have you ever looked through a magnifying glass? A magnifying glass makes things look bigger so we can see them better. That's what God's beautiful world does. It is like a magnifying glass that magnifies God so we can see Him better. When we study the flowers -- their beauty and how perfectly they were created -- we know that God is beautiful, perfect, and creative. God is *very* creative. He must have an incredible imagination. Do you have an imagination? Of course you do, because you were made in the image of God! You have also been given many of the other wonderful traits that He has. Since your creativity shows us that you were made in the image of God, it magnifies God when you do creative things.

As we study nature and all that God created with such amazing and complex design, we become even more amazed about God. It blesses and pleases God for us to wonder at the work of His hands. As we study plants this year, we will know and understand God better and better. He will be magnified to us through the study of His creation.

Latin

Were you named after someone or someplace special? Was your mother or father named after anyone? What about your grandparents? Ask your parents who they were named after. It is interesting to learn where names come from. Do you like to know why things are named the way they are? If so, you will enjoy this book, because we are going to look at the meanings behind a lot of words. We are also going to find out why certain things are named the way they are. A lot of words used in science come from a language called **Latin**. Latin is often called a dead language, because no one speaks it anymore. Of course, people did speak it at one time. For example, the ancient Romans spoke Latin. Do you know who the ancient Romans were? They were the people who wore togas and put wreaths around their heads.

Why do scientists use Latin? Well, suppose I wanted to make a certain medicine that they make in Egypt. Some medicines are made from plants, so let's assume that's how they make this medicine. To make the medicine, then, I would need to know which plants to use. How could I know which plants the Egyptians use to make the medicine unless we call the plants by the same names? Scientists like to discuss things with people from other countries, and since every nation has a different name for the same plant, we need to have a name that is the same for everyone. Since no one in the world speaks Latin as their main language, Latin never changes! This makes Latin a great language to use for scientific names. That way, the names are the same for everyone, and they never change.

Many of our words come from the Latin language. Studying Latin makes it easier to know the meaning of words in our own language. Studying Latin also makes it easier to learn other languages. If you are planning to be a scientist when you grow up, you may want to learn Latin. We are going to learn some Latin words in this lesson. You don't have to remember them all unless you want to. You can jot them down in your notebook as you hear them, if you like.

Botanists

Botanists study plants.

Have you ever heard the word **biology** (by ahl' uh jee)? It sounds like a complicated word, but "biology" just means "the study of living things." You will learn biology in this course, since plants are living things. Even though a lot of scientific words come from Latin, many come from Greek. Biology is one example. In Greek, **bio** means **life** and **ology** means **the study of**. So "biology" is "the study of life, or living things." People who study biology are called **biologists** (by ahl' uh jists). As I said before, the study of plants is called botany. That comes from the Greek word **botane**, which means **plant**. A botanist is a biologist who studies plants.

So what do botanists actually do? Well, have you ever taken medicine that made you well? Some botanists study plants that can be used to make medicines which cure disease. Many different medicines are made from plants. Other botanists experiment with plants to learn more about them. Some of these botanists have grown plants inside space stations like the one in the picture. They do this to learn about gravity and how it affects plants. They are called **astrobiologists** (as' troh by ahl' uh jists): astronauts who study living things. That blue, cloudy looking ocean below the space station is actually the planet earth as we see it from

This is a picture of the Skylab space station in orbit around the earth.

space. Would you like to be an astrobiologist? Experimenting with plants is very exciting, even if you aren't up in a space ship. We will do many experiments with plants in this book. You will even grow your own herbs and make herbal soap from them!

Taxonomy

Do you like to have things organized? Do you like it when all your shirts are in one drawer, your socks are in another drawer, and your pants in a different drawer? It makes life a lot easier when we are organized. Well, biologists like to organize living things. God created so many different living things that biologists have spent a great deal of time separating them into different groups, called **kingdoms**. This helps biologists keep things organized. They put plants in one huge group, called kingdom **Plantae** (plan' tay), and animals in another huge group, called kingdom Animalia (an uh mal' ee uh). There are three other kingdoms: one for mushrooms and other similar living things called kingdom Fungi (fun' jye), one for teeny-tiny bacteria called Monera (muh nihr' uh), and one for other microscopic living things called Protista (pro tee' stuh). Which kingdom do you think this book is about? It's about kingdom Plantae, of course!

Kingdom Plantae includes all the plants on the earth. That's a big kingdom. To make this kingdom easier to study, each plant is put into a smaller group called a **phylum** (fie' lum). We are going to study a few phyla ("phyla" means "more than one phylum") of kingdom Plantae in this book. If you were going to separate all the plants on earth into different phyla, how would you do it? How about putting all the plants that make flowers in one phylum? What about plants that grow pinecones? Would you put all the cone-making plants in their own phylum? This is exactly what scientists do. The process of placing things into groups is called **classification**.

Putting plants into different phyla helps organize the plants for those who study them, but that's not enough. There are just too many plants to organize. Because of this, scientists have broken plants into even smaller groups, which they then break into even smaller groups, which they then break into even smaller groups, and so on. This process is sort of like dividing up all your Legos® into groups by their size, shape, color, and purpose. To do this, you would just keep making the groups smaller and smaller until you have lots of little groups of Legos. Each group of Legos would be made up of Legos that are exactly alike. If you start with a very large Lego collection, that could take a long time.

Classifying plants is a lot like organizing Legos.

Once a plant has been classified or put into a phylum, it is then put into a smaller group called a **class**, and then it is put into a smaller group called an **order**. That's not the end of it, however. The plant is then put into a **family**, then a **genus** (jee' nus), and finally a **species** (spee' sheez). Wow! This whole business of dividing plants up into different groups and naming each group is hard work, and it is called **taxonomy** (tax on' uh me). Some people love organizing and classifying living things so much that they grow up to be taxonomists, scientists whose job is to classify living things.

To help you understand taxonomy, let's look at an example. Suppose you decided to classify all of the people who go to your church. You could start by naming five kingdoms: married adults, single adults, teenagers, young students, and preschoolers. Then, you could separate each kingdom into different phyla based on the person's age. Preschoolers could be broken up into one year olds, two year olds, three year olds, and four year olds. Married adults could be broken up into 20 year olds, 30 year olds, 40 year olds, etc. You could then separate the phyla into two classes: males and females. You could then separate the classes into orders based on the color of the person's eyes. You could further break the orders into families by separating the people by the city in which they live. To put each person into a genus, you could separate them by their last name. Finally, to put each person into a species, you could separate people by their first names. If you did this, what would be the taxonomy for Jordan Smith, a two-year-old boy with blue eyes from New York City? It would be **kingdom**: preschoolers; **phylum**: two year olds; **class**: male; **order**: blue eyes; **family**: New York City; **genus**: *Smith*; **species**: *Jordan*.

Once botanists have placed the plants into groups by their special features, they give the plant two names: one based on its genus, and one based on its species. If we did this for the boy above, we would call him *Smith jordan*. When you name things the way botanists do, you put both the genus and the species in italics, and you capitalize the genus name but not the species name.

When you name things this way, you are using **binomial** (by no' me uhl) **nomenclature** (no' men klay' chur). Those are two giant words, but they are not too hard to understand when you see where they come from. **Bi** means **two**; **nome** means **name**; and **clature** means **to assign.** So **binomial** means **two names**, and **nomenclature** means **name assigning**. Binomial nomenclature, then, means assigning two names. That's what botanists (and all scientists who study living things) do. They give two names to each living thing. Guess what language the names are usually in? Latin, of course! How many times do you think you can quickly say "binomial nomenclature"? It's a tongue twister!

Next time you read about a plant, you might see two Latin words in italics next to its English name. That's its scientific name, written in binomial nomenclature. If you have an encyclopedia, look up a plant that you have or know about. See if the encyclopedia gives its scientific name, and if it does, try to pronounce it.

What Do You Remember?

What is biology? What is botany? Are all botanists biologists? Are all biologists botanists? Why do scientists use Latin? What is taxonomy? What is binomial nomenclature?

Notebook Activities

You will keep a special botany notebook throughout this study. Take care as you write and

draw in the pages of this notebook. Do your very best so that at the end of the year you can look back over your work and be proud of what you have accomplished. You will also collect specimens for this notebook. That means you will put things from nature (like leaves and flowers) into your notebook. When you do this, be sure to take only one of each specimen. It is important to study nature by collecting specimens, but if you take too many specimens, it could have a bad effect on other living things in the area.

You can add anything you like to your botany notebook. Whenever you go to a park or outdoors, take a writing tablet so that you can draw and write about what you see. Those drawings and writings could go into your notebook. Also, you could take a specimen for your notebook that relates to something you have just studied. When you bring the specimen home, be certain to label it for your notebook. Your notebook will be a great reminder of all that you learned this year, and you can use it to teach others about the wonders of botany.

Older Students: Write down everything you have learned so far about botany. Then make an illustration that will be the cover page for your botany notebook. After that, you can do the following activity to help you remember what taxonomy is.

Younger Students: Tell your parent / teacher everything you have learned so far about botany so that she can write it down in your notebook. Make an illustration that will be the cover page for your botany notebook. After that, you can do the following activity to help you remember what taxonomy is.

Taxonomy Exercise: Shoe Taxonomy

Today you are going to get hands-on experience as a taxonomist. Taxonomists usually group and name living things, but you will be a shoe taxonomist. In order to do this, gather one of every shoe in your house. If you are doing this in a classroom environment, each child should take off one shoe and put it in a pile on the floor. This activity will require a lot of deep thinking as you try to figure out how to classify the shoes.

You should pick about four kingdoms for your shoe taxonomy, two phyla for each kingdom, two classes for each division, and two orders for each class. To get started, study all the different shoes. What big differences separate each of the shoes? The largest differences can be used to separate the shoes into kingdoms. Is it worn only to special places or events? Is it an everyday shoe? How do you put it on? When you have decided on four kingdoms, separate the shoes into kingdoms and look at them. What is different about each shoe in each kingdom? Continue separating the shoes like this until you get down to a class for each shoe.

Older Students: If you have enough shoes, take your taxonomy all the way down to species by making at least two families for each class, two genera (jahn' er uh - "genera" means "more than one genus") for each family, and two species for each genus.

When you get done, write down the name of each shoe using binomial nomenclature. Put your classification system on a chart. If you have a camera, you could take a picture of this activity and put it in your notebook! In case you are having trouble with this activity, look at the "Answers to the Narrative Questions" section near the back of the book. You will find a sample classification system there. That should help you.

Phyla

Did you enjoy the shoe activity? What kinds of things did you look for when putting shoes into different phyla? Would you like to learn what botanists look for to separate the plants into phyla? One thing they look for is whether or not plants have tubes inside them. Do you have tubes inside of you? We'll find out in a minute. Another thing botanists look at is how the seeds are made. Do you make seeds? No, you don't. As you study this course, you will see that God made humans and plants very different but at the same time very similar. Let's explore these two things (tubes and seed-making), since they are important features in plants.

Vascular Plants

Vascular (vask' you luhr) plants have tubes that carry liquid inside the plant. The word "vascular" means "tubes that carry fluid." Fluid is just another word for liquid, which is anything that has the same form as water. Most liquids are wet when we touch them. What liquid do you think runs inside the tubes of a plant? We'll find out in just a minute.

Did you know that you have tubes inside your body? Look at your wrist. Do you see blue streaks? Those are tubes that we call **veins** (vaynes). They contain a fluid. What do you think that fluid is called? It's called blood, of course! You see, then, that you and I are vascular, just like some plants. Almost every part of your body is vascular, which means it is filled with tubes that carry blood. Some of the tubes (like the ones you see in your wrist) are veins, and others are called **arteries** (ar' tur ees). Have you ever noticed that when you cut yourself, you bleed? That's because there are arteries and veins underneath your skin. If you cut your skin deeply enough, those arteries and veins get cut, and the blood inside them spills out.

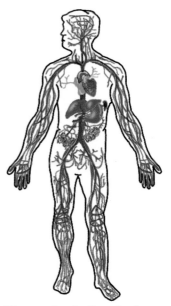

The arteries (red) and veins (blue) in our bodies are called "vascular tissue."

God made many living things in a similar way; plants and people both have tubes inside them. This shows us that God is consistent in His design of the world. Think about the pictures you draw. All of the pictures you draw are similar to one another because they are made by the same artist: you. That is how it is with God's world. He made many living things with tubes inside them. Not all living things have tubes inside them, but many do. We can see that everything in the world was made by the same artist: God!

Although the tubes in our body are somewhat similar to the tubes in plant, plant tubes don't have blood running through them. Did you guess that plant tubes have water moving through them?

That's right! There's more than just water, however. There are also chemicals in the water. Water and these chemicals run up the plant in tubes called **xylem** (zy' lum). Sugar and other chemicals flow down the plant through other tubes called **phloem** (floh' em). We'll learn all about xylem and phloem in a later lesson. The whole plant has these tubes. Look at the flower in the picture to the right. Do you see the tubes? When we see tubes in a flower or plant, we usually call them "veins," even though they do not carry blood. Although you can actually see many of the tubes in a plant by just looking at its leaves or flowers, many are also hidden inside the plant and are hard to see.

The veins in these flowers are easy to see.

Try This!

Get a leaf from a nearby plant. Look at it very carefully. What do you see? You should see lines running through the leaf. Those lines are the veins that carry water through the leaf. Do you see one vein in the very middle that is thicker than the rest? That's called the **midrib**. It gets water from the stem and carries it to all of the smaller veins in the leaf. Did you know that there are even more veins under the green part of the leaf? They are hard to see right now. In a later lesson, however, you will do an experiment that takes all the green stuff off the leaf to expose the hidden veins beneath. In other words, you will skin a leaf in a later lesson!

In this leaf, the veins and the midrib are easy to see.

Save your leaf to put in your notebook. The best thing to do is glue it to a piece of paper with white school and let it dry. After the glue dries, stick it in a page protector and put it in your notebook. Write down what you have learned so far and put that in your notebook with the leaf.

What Do You Remember?

Pause a moment and explain in your own words what makes a plant a vascular plant. What does the vascular system of a plant do? What does your vascular system do? What else have you learned so far?

Nonvascular Plants

Most plants have veins, so most plants are vascular. In fact, if a plant has roots, stems, and leaves, it is a vascular plant. Can you think of any plant that doesn't have stems, roots, and leaves? There are only a few, and they are called **nonvascular** plants, because they do not have tubes inside them. It's hard to imagine plants without stems, roots, and leaves, but they do exist! In fact, you probably have some growing near your home.

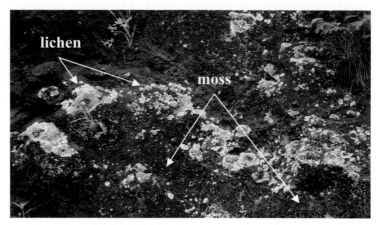

Moss that grows on rocks and trees is a nonvascular plant. If you study these plants, they look like they might have leaves or stems, but they aren't *true* leaves and stems because they do not have tubes inside them. **Lichens** (like' un), those little plant-like clumps that grow on rocks, look like

Lichen and moss can grow on rocks.

nonvascular plants, but they are not. They are actually two living things rolled up into one!   You will learn more about them in a little while.

Nonvascular plants have a different way of moving water through the plant. They simply absorb water and spread it around as much of the plant as they can, the way a paper towel does.

Paper Towel Activity

Here's an activity to help you understand how nonvascular plants get the water they need to survive. You will need a paper towel and some water. Do you think a paper towel has veins or tubes inside of it to transport water? No, it doesn't. It absorbs water. That's how it gets wet all over.

Spill some water on a counter and place the edge of the paper towel in the water. Notice how the water spreads through the paper towel. If there is enough water, a lot of the paper towel will get wet. If not, only a small part of it will get wet. That's similar to the way moss and other nonvascular plants get the water they need. They need to have a lot of water present in order to get the water spread throughout the whole plant. If they don't get enough water, they will dry up. Places that have a lot of humidity (which is water vapor floating in the air around you) have a lot of nonvascular plants. Why? Well, if there is a lot of water present in the air, the plants have access to a great deal of water and can grow and survive easily.

Moss

If you can find any moss growing outside, get a magnifying glass and look at it closely. You may be surprised at its appearance. You will notice that it looks like it might have a stem or little leaves. But they are not true leaves with a vascular system. They have no tubes inside.

Try to draw the moss you see for your notebook. Write down what you have learned so far about nonvascular plants.

Moss growing on a rock can be a beautiful sight.

Seed Homes

Do you remember the other thing a botanist looks at when classifying plants? It is way the plant makes seeds. Seeds are like baby plants inside a little house. What kind of home are seeds born in? Some seeds are formed inside a vessel. Look at the peanut in the picture on the left. A peanut is made of an outer shell that is called a **pod**. That's the vessel that holds the seeds. When you peel away the pod, you usually find two ovals inside. Those are the seeds. When we eat peanuts, we eat the seeds of the peanut plant.

seeds

top part of the pod

Botanists classify plants based on whether or not they make seeds. Plants that do make seeds are further divided into how they make their seeds. We will start by studying the plants that make seeds, and then we will study the plants that do not. There are two different kinds of plants that make seeds: **angiosperms** (an' jee oh spurms) and **gymnosperms** (jim' no spurms). These kinds of plants are separated into different phyla, depending on *how* they make their seeds. You will understand what I mean when we start studying the phyla.

We are going to look at several plant phyla and learn their names. If you enjoy learning where words come from, you will enjoy the rest of this lesson. We will be learning a lot of Greek and Latin names and what they mean.

Angiosperms
Phylum Anthophyta

Do you like flowers? I bet you do.
Most people enjoy looking at a garden full of
flowers.   That is just the way God made us.
Since we are made in His image, I bet He enjoys
looking at flowers too! That's reason enough to
plant a garden, isn't it?

Flower-making plants are put in one
giant phylum called **Anthophyta** (an' thoh fie'
tuh). If you know Greek, it is easy to
understand where this word comes from,
because **antho** means **flower** and **phyta** means **plant**. This tells us that the plants in phylum
Anthophyta are the plants that make flowers. They are also called angiosperms. **Angio** means
container, and **sperm** is another word for **seed**. **Angiosperm**, then, means **seed container**.

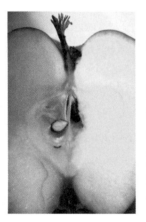

I bet you figured out that seeds of angiosperms are inside of some kind of
container. What kind of container? Well, that depends. We don't usually think
of fruit as a container, but that is exactly what it is: a container for seeds! Some
plants make a prickly sticker for their seeds, while others make a container with
a furry parachute attached so that the seeds can go flying in the wind. God
created many different kinds of containers for the seeds of angiosperms. Can
you think of any seed containers that you have seen? Did you know that an
apple is a container for apple seeds? Nuts and acorns are containers for seeds
that could one day be giant trees.

Did you know that before the apple, pea pod, or acorn
showed up on the plant there was a flower there first? All
angiosperms make flowers before they make their seeds. The
best way to figure out if a plant is an angiosperm is to ask
yourself, "Does it make flowers?" If you can answer "yes,"
the plant is an angiosperm. In fact, the whole purpose of the
flower is to make seeds. The flower actually contains the
stuff needed to make seeds. Then, when the flower gets
pollinated, the petals fall off, and the part that is left begins to
get really fat. This swelling structure begins to form into a
container for the seeds. We will learn all about this amazing process soon.

A cactus is an angiosperm, because it makes
flowers.

What Do You Remember?

Can you tell someone in your own words what angiosperms are? What does angiosperm mean? In which phylum do botanists put the angiosperms? What does the name of the phylum mean? What is the purpose of a flower?

Gymnosperms
Phylum Coniferophyta

If a seed-making plant is not an angiosperm, it is a gymnosperm. **Gymno** means **uncovered**, and as I told you already, **sperm** is another word for **seed**. This tells us that **gymnosperm** means **uncovered seed**. What does that tell us about the seeds that are made by gymnosperms? They are not covered up when they are being made. Remember, angiosperms produce seeds that are in some kind of container. That means they are covered up. Gymnosperm seeds are not.

Botanists separate gymnosperms into four different phyla. We are going to discuss only one of them – the one that has the most plants in it. That phylum is called **Coniferophyta** (con ih' fur oh fye' tuh). **Conifer** is Latin for **cone bearer**, and as I told you before, **phyta** means **plant**. This tells us that coniferophyta are cone-bearing plants. Can you think of a cone-bearing plant? Have you ever seen a pinecone? The pinecone is kind of like the "flower" of an evergreen (pine) tree, because that's where the seeds of an evergreen tree are formed. Botanists are very careful not to call pinecones flowers, however, because they are not flowers.

Pine trees are in phylum Coniferophyta, because they produce pinecones.

Are there any cone-making plants in your neighborhood? Well, if you can see pine trees in your neighborhood, then there are cone-making plants there, because pine trees are in phylum Coniferophyta! If you look at a cone that comes from a pine tree, you might see tiny seeds inside. Pine trees grow from those tiny seeds. Even the tallest trees in the world, the redwoods in California, start out as one of these tiny little seeds. Isn't God's creation incredible? We will do some experiments with pinecones in a later lesson. If you happen to find a pinecone, save it so you can use it in that experiment.

Seedless Vascular Plants
Phylum Pterophyta

Have you ever seen a plant called a fern? Ferns are from a phylum called **Pterophyta** (tare uh fie' tuh). Have you ever heard of a dinosaur called a pterodactyl (tare uh dak' tuhl)? It's a flying dinosaur. You see, **ptero** comes from Greek and means **wing**. As I told you before, **phyta** means **plant**. A fern, then, is a "wing plant." Can you guess why a fern is called that? Look at the fern pictured on the right. A fern's frond, or leaf, sure does look like a wing, doesn't it? Botanists sometimes use names that describe what they think a plant looks like. Since fern

The leaves on a fern look something like green feathers.

leaves look like wings, botanists call ferns "wing plants," which puts them in phylum Pterophyta.

clumps
of spores

Each of the clumps on this fern contains millions of spores.

Ferns are vascular. Do you remember what it means for a plant to be vascular? It means that the plant has tubes inside it. However, these plants do not make seeds. They make **sporangia** (spuh ran' jee uh). **Angia,** just like angio, means **container**. This tells us that **sporangia** means **spore container**. Seedless vascular plants like ferns don't make flowers or cones. They don't make seeds, either. They make little balls called sporangia that are filled with spores. These spores can one day grow into a new plant.

Even though seeds and spores both grow into plants, spores are not seeds. You see, a seed is a very special package. It contains a baby plant, food for the baby plant, and a protective covering. You can think of a seed as a baby plant in a box with its lunch. A spore is just the baby plant and a protective coating. There is no food for the baby plant. Since there is no food in a spore, spores are much smaller than seeds.

You can think of ferns as spore-makers, not flower-makers. They never, ever make flowers. Can you remember the purpose of a flower? Why do you think a fern doesn't make flowers? It doesn't need to, because it doesn't need to make seeds. Instead, it makes spores.

Nonvascular Plants
Phylum Bryophyta

This moss is growing on a rock that is in a stream.

Now it's time to talk about the **nonvascular plants**. Remember what nonvascular means. It means that there are no tubes in the plant. That means the plant must absorb water like a paper towel. As I mentioned before, this means that these kinds of plants need lots of water. Look at the moss growing on the rock in the picture on the left. That's an ideal place for a nonvascular plant, because there is a lot of water running over the rock. Nonvascular plants do not make seeds. Like ferns, they make sporangia, which are filled with spores that can grow into new plants. Unlike ferns, however, they do not have tubes inside them. Mosses are nonvascular plants.

Mosses are everywhere. Even though they require a lot of water, they can withstand long, dry spells. Because of this, you can even find mosses in the desert! There are so many mosses that they have their own phylum, called **Bryophyta** (bry oh fie' tuh). **Bryo** comes from Greek and means **moss**. Phylum Bryophyta, then, contains the "moss plants."

As I mentioned earlier, some people mistake lichens for moss-like plants because you can sometimes find lichens growing where you find moss growing. However, lichens are not really plants. They are actually two living things rolled up into one! A **fungus** plus **algae** (al' jee) makes lichen. If you don't know what fungus is, a mushroom is an example of a fungus. Algae, on the other hand, are so small that you usually need a microscope to see them. They usually live in water, but sometimes, they team up with a fungus to become a lichen. The fungus draws up water and certain chemicals that the algae needs, and the algae makes food for both of them. Fungus and algae make a very interesting "team," don't you think?

This lichen is growing on a dead tree.

Lichens grow in places that have clean air, and the cleaner the air, the greener the lichens. If you see a lot of lichens growing on trees or rocks in a certain place, take a deep breath of the squeaky clean air! If you are interested, there is a great idea for a science fair project using lichen at the end of Lesson 12.

What Do You Remember?

Name something you remember about angiosperms. What are gymnosperms? What does the word "coniferophyta" mean? What do ferns and mosses have in common? What is different between ferns and mosses? What is the phylum for ferns? What is the phylum for mosses?

Notebook Activity

Today you are going to make some drawings from nature. You will take four sheets of paper and write ANGIOSPERM on the top of one, GYMNOSPERM on another, SEEDLESS VASCULAR PLANT on another and NONVASCULAR PLANT on the last. Go back through the lesson to remind yourself of each phylum we studied and write the correct phylum name on each sheet of paper.

Go outside and sketch one of each of these types of plants. If you cannot find one or more of these types of plants, you can look through books or search the internet to find a picture of one to draw. Place your finished work in your notebook.

Older Students: Next to your sketch, write down the features of each plant which cause it to be classified in that group.

Project
Making a Light Hut and Growing Herbs

After every lesson in this course, there will be at least one project for you to do. Often, it will be to grow plants, but there are many other fun things you will do as well. Most of your projects will take a few days to complete. For this lesson, you will begin growing herbs inside a light hut. Later on, you will make home-made soap with these herbs. You can also use the herbs for cooking.

You need to start by building a small light hut. You will then use the light hut to start growing your own plants. It will be a fun place to care for your plants before they are ready to be transplanted into a pot or outside. You can choose many different plants to put inside your light hut! Though you can choose any plants you want to grow, I will give some suggestions for good herbs to grow for the soap you will make. Your light hut will be a perfect environment to grow many varieties of plants. Because you will use a fluorescent light, the light hut will not use much energy and can be kept on all the time. This will help your plants grow faster.

Light Hut

You will need:

- An empty "copy paper" box, or shipping box
- Aluminum foil (approximately 10-15 feet)
- Electrical cord
- A light socket with plug
- Plastic plate or lid (such as the lid to an oatmeal, large yogurt, or sour cream container)
- Glue
- Scissors
- A 15-watt fluorescent spiral light (Most stores such as Wal-Mart carry these lights.)

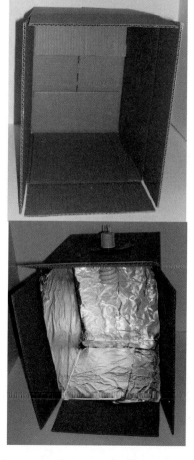

1. Cut a 1-inch hole in the center of the plastic plate or lid and trim off the edges to make a 4- to 5-inch disk with a 1-inch center hole.
2. Stand the box on its side as shown on the right.
3. Cut a 1-inch hole in the top center of box.
4. Cut ventilation slots in the top, upper sides, and back of the box to allow air flow and to allow heat to escape.
5. Use glue and aluminum foil to cover the entire inside of the box with aluminum foil. This will make the inside of the box very shiny.
6. Cut a hole through the aluminum foil where the hole in the top of the box is, and cut slits in the foil where the ventilation slots are.
7. Push the base of the light (without the socket attached) through hole in top of the box.
8. Put the plastic plate on the box so that the base of the light sticks through its hole as well.
9. Secure the light by attaching the socket from the outside of the box. See the picture to the right.
10. Tape an aluminum foil curtain to the top front edge of box so that it hangs down over the opening of the box. See the picture on the next page. This curtain is designed to keep light from escaping the box. However, it needs to hang loosely so that there is plenty of ventilation. If your plants seem to dry out or if the inside of the box gets hot, you might want to remove the curtain.

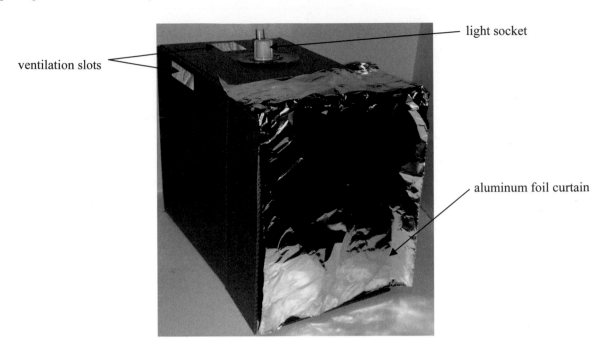

light socket

ventilation slots

aluminum foil curtain

What to Plant

You can buy seeds through seed companies online or at any store in the spring. In addition to herbs for soap and cooking, grow some fruits and vegetables that your family can eat. Also, you might want to grow squash to help with an activity in Lesson 4. An acorn squash is particularly fun, because you can make it into a bird house.

Herbs

Growing herbs can be extremely rewarding. You will be surprised at the many uses for herbs. If you are an older student, you might want to do some research on the use of herbs throughout history. You will learn many interesting facts.

The herbs we most enjoy are those that give a strong aroma and can be eaten. You will grow herbs to put in home-made soap. Herbal soaps and teas make great gifts and can be given away or even sold. I will give instructions for growing herbs and making soap below.

Herbs that smell especially nice and can be used in tea are: lavender (*Lavandula angustifolia*), spearmint (*Mentha spicata)*, peppermint (*Mentha piperita*), and chamomile *(Chamaemelum nobile)*.

You can even create your own tea bags out of coffee filters and a staple, modeled after store-bought tea bags.

To grow herbs for making soap, choose herbs that are good for the skin: lemon balm (*Melissa officinalis)*, calendula (*Calendula officinalis)*, Russian comfrey (*Symphytum x uplandicum)*, catnip (*Nepeta cataria*), and basil (*Ocimum basilicum*).

Growing the Plants

You will need:

♦ Peat moss
♦ Seeds for the plants you have decided to grow
♦ Containers for your plants (Styrofoam cups will work, but small plant pots are ideal.)
♦ Saucers or plastic lids
♦ Small paper bags
♦ String
♦ Scissors

1. Make sure the containers you use have drainage holes in the bottom. If they do not, make some.
2. Plant your seeds in peat moss in the containers.
3. To make the plants grow strong and healthy, keep them in your light hut. Put them on saucers or plastic lids so that the water that drains through the drainage holes doesn't spill everywhere. Keep the light hut on 24 hours a day.
4. Water your seeds daily. The roots need oxygen, just like you and me, so don't pour too much water on them. If you pour too much water on them, you will drown your plants. Make sure you have drain holes and a little saucer or plastic lid underneath so that water can escape. If the soil feels moist to the touch, your plants don't need water. If the soil is so wet that the dirt sticks to your finger, your plants might have too much water and not enough drainage holes. If the soil feels dry, give your plants some water.
5. If a plant gets too large for your light hut, move it to a sunny spot outdoors or to a large pot by a sunny window. You might have to transplant it to a bigger pot. If you live in a region that does not get much sun, you can create an additional, larger light hut for your growing plants.
6. The flowers of some herbs (like lavender) are useful, while the leaves of other herbs (like basil) are used. When the plants have grown to produce useful leaves or flowers, harvest them.
7. After harvesting, lightly rinse the herbs. You will need to do the next steps right away. If you wait after harvesting the herbs, they might decay rather than dry.
8. Cut off the dead or discolored leaves or stems.
9. Tie the stems together and hang them upside down in a small brown paper bag that has ventilation holes cut into it.
10. Make sure they are hung in a dry, well-ventilated area. They should dry in five to 10 days.
11. Once they are dry, you can use them in cooking or to make soap.

Making Soap

You will need:

- Glycerin soap bars for soap making (You can order these from any soap-making supplies store. It is safer to buy these rather than to make them from scratch, because making them from scratch requires lye, which can be dangerous if used carelessly.)
- Glass measuring cup or bowl
- Soap mold (A disposable plastic container works great, but fancy molds are available for a few dollars at any craft store.)
- Olive oil or Vaseline®
- Dried herbs that you grew, and any other additives such as *Aloe vera*, vitamin E, cold-pressed olive oil, or ground oatmeal
- Craft sticks for stirring
- Fragrance: essential oils or fragrance oils found at health food stores
- Microwave or double boiler

1. Have an adult cut the glycerin soap bars into 1-inch chunks or grate them with a cheese grater. Place the grated or cut bars into the glass measuring cup.
2. Microwave for 20-30 second at a time until all of the chunks are melted. Do not boil! You can also do this in a double boiler.
3. When the soap cools a bit (but before it begins to set) start adding your herbs, fragrances, and other ingredients. Use about ½ teaspoon of each herb per cup of soap. You will probably have to experiment with how much of the fragrances and other ingredients to add, but ½ teaspoon per cup of soap is a reasonable amount to try for anything you are adding to the soap. Avoid adding the herbs and fragrance while the soap is too hot, because the scent may burn off from the heat of the soap. Don't wait too long, however, because the soap will begin to set up and form a top skin.
4. Stir with wooden craft sticks.
5. Put your mold on a level surface, and coat the inside of it with olive oil or Vaseline.
6. Once you have mixed your herbs into the soap, pour the soap into your soap mold.
7. Let your soap cool until it is hardened. You can put your mold in the freezer to speed up this process.
8. Remove the soap from the mold.
9. Air-dry your soap on a rack or wax paper overnight.
10. Wrap your soap in cellophane to preserve the aroma.
11. If you plan to give the soap as a gift, make a nice label and tie ribbons around the cellophane.

Lesson 2
Seeds

Note to the teacher: For the first portion of this lesson, you will need a magnifying glass, a sunflower seed, and several bean seeds. Begin soaking a few of the bean seeds in hot water 30 minutes before you begin the lesson.

Did you know that inside every seed is a tiny living thing? That living thing is a little baby plant, fast asleep. A baby plant doesn't sleep the way you and I do. It is a different kind of sleep. We say that the plant is **dormant**. The word dormant comes from the Latin word **dormire**, which means **to sleep**. The baby plant stays dormant until it gets what it needs to wake up. When it wakes up, it begins to grow into a little plant called a **seedling**. When it does this, it uses the soft fleshy material inside the seed for food until it is ready to make food on its own using sunlight, water, and air.

What do you think the baby plant needs to wake up? Make some guesses. There are really only three things the baby plant needs to wake up: warmth, water, and air. You might think that it needs soil, but it doesn't. The plant will not use the chemicals found in soil for a few days or weeks, because the seed itself has everything it needs to begin growing. You might think that a baby plant needs sunlight to wake up and begin growing, but it doesn't. In fact, many seeds begin growing underground where there is no sunlight at all. A seed only needs warmth, water, and air to wake up. Later on, it will begin to need sunlight. If there is sunlight present, the plant will use it to grow nice and healthy. If there is no sunlight present, the plant will grow anyway, but it will grow differently. It won't be as

Each of these sunflower seeds contains a baby plant, the plant's food, and a protective coating. The seeds need only warmth, water, and air to begin to grow into beautiful sunflowers.

healthy. Its stem will grow longer and longer, searching for sunlight. If it never finds the sunlight, it will eventually die, because it needs light to make food for itself once the food in the seed runs out.

When the temperature is just right and there is water and air present, the baby plant begins to emerge from inside of the seed. If the temperature is not warm enough, or there is no water or air, the baby plant will stay snuggled inside its seed, fast asleep. Do you ever feel like staying in bed under your covers? A baby plant will stay under its covers until it has what it needs to grow.

Sometimes, a baby plant sleeps for a few weeks inside its seed. Can you imagine sleeping for a few weeks? Sometimes, a baby plant can sleep for years! Believe it or not, it can even sleep for thousands of years, if it must! Now that's a long sleep, isn't it? How do we know that a baby plant can sleep for thousands of years inside its seed? Well, there was once a king in Egypt named Tutankhamen (toot' un kah' muhn). We call him King Tut. He lived about 1,300 years before Jesus was born. That was more than 3,000 years ago! One day, not so very long ago, scientists found King Tut's tomb. Do you know what a tomb is? A tomb is a place where people bury their dead. Inside the tomb was a jar of bean seeds! The baby plants inside the bean seeds had been dormant for more than 3,000 years! Do you think they could still grow after all of that time? Well, the scientists took them home and planted them, and guess what? They grew! They grew into lovely bean plants. The bean plants even made seeds that grew into new bean plants. To this day, there are people growing bean plants that originally started with King Tut's bean seeds!

King Tut's burial mask was recovered from his tomb.

Seeds are one of God's most special and important creations. It is amazing that inside of every seed is a baby plant waiting to awaken and become a grown plant. The baby inside the plant is called an **embryo** (em' bree oh). Did you know that you were once an embryo? When you were inside your mother's womb, you were a little embryo. Of course, you weren't a plant embryo, and you didn't act like one either! You weren't dormant; you were wide awake most of the time. You were actively moving, jumping, and kicking. As you grew, you opened your eyes, sucked your thumb, and even had the hic-ups every now and then. There was a certain time when you would come out. No matter what, you were coming out in about nine months. There was no way you were going to wait 3,000 years before you came out into the world!

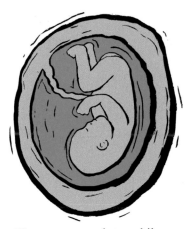

You were an embryo while you were growing in your mother's womb.

God created humans and plants very differently, but we see the signs of the same Creator in both humans and plants, don't we? We all begin as embryos, and we all begin protected inside something. Your mother's womb protected you when you were an embryo. What protects a plant embryo? Can you guess? Did you guess the shell of the seed? That's right, and now it's time for you to learn more about a seed's shell.

Testas

If you have a bean seed and a sunflower seed, get them now. Look at the shells of your seeds. The shell, or coat, of a seed is called the **testa** (test' uh). The testa protects the embryo, much like a winter coat protects a person from a cold winter's chill. What color is your winter coat? Wouldn't it be strange if everyone in the world had the exact same coat? That would be kind of boring, wouldn't it? Well, God must not like things to be boring, because He gave different coats to every seed He made. This means each plant's seed has a different testa.

Look at your sunflower seed. What color is its testa? Is it striped? Is your coat striped? What color is the bean seed's testa? Do you know what an acorn testa looks like? An acorn has a little "hat" to go along with its winter coat, doesn't it? Have you ever seen the seed that a palm tree makes? They are called coconuts, and they have a very interesting testa! Testas come in all different shapes, sizes, and colors. Seeds from some plants have thin testas, like a spring jacket. Seeds from other plants have testas that are thick and strong, like an Eskimo's coat. The walnut seed's testa is wrinkly and very strong. Coconut seed testas are strong, brown, and "furry." Corn seed testas are thin, smooth, and yellow. Lima bean testas are thin, smooth, and white. God designed so many interesting testas when He filled the world with seeds. Do you remember the seeds that you planted in your light hut? What did their testas look like? Were they all the same shape? Were they all the same color? Were they all the same size?

A coconut is the seed of a palm tree. Its testa is brown and "furry."

Take Off Your Coat!

When your coat gets wet or when it's warm outside, do you take it off? Well, that's what the seed does when its coat gets wet and warm. When the seed is soaked in water, such as after a warm spring rain, the testa gets waterlogged and soggy. The testa then comes off, and the sleeping embryo gets the water.

Look closely at the bean testa with a magnifying glass. In the curve of the bean seed there is a little "scar." That's the seed's belly button! Every seed has a belly button. It's actually called a **hilum** (high' lum), and it is where the seed was attached to its mother. You have a belly button as well, and it is also the place

bean seed hilum   sunflower seed hilum

where you were attached to your mother. Can you find the hilum on the sunflower seed? It's not on the pointed end; it's on the other end of the sunflower seed.

What Do You Remember?

What is a seed? What does "dormant" mean? What does a seed need to wake up and begin growing? What is the baby plant in a seed called? What is the seed's testa? What does it do? What is the hilum on a seed?

Activity
Open a Seed

Would you like to see a plant embryo for yourself? Do you have a bean seed that has been soaking in warm water? If so, get it now. Examine the seed. Do you see how wrinkled the testa is? It is wrinkled because it absorbed water and began to detach from the seed. This allowed the water to get into the seed so that the embryo could begin to grow.

Now pull apart your seed very slowly and carefully. If you were very careful, you will see a tiny growth inside of the seed. Look closely. Doesn't it almost look like a tiny plant? That is part of the embryo! Study it with a magnifying glass.

There are five main parts to the embryo in your seed: the **cotyledons** (kot' uh lee' dunz), the **radicle** (rad' ih cul), the **hypocotyl** (hi' puh kot' uhl), the **epicotyl** (ep' uh kot' uhl), and the **plumule** (ploom' yool). Can you find and point to these parts on your embryo? You might not be able to see the plumule, because it might have been broken off when you pulled the seed apart. Now that you know the five main parts, you can learn a little bit about what these parts do.

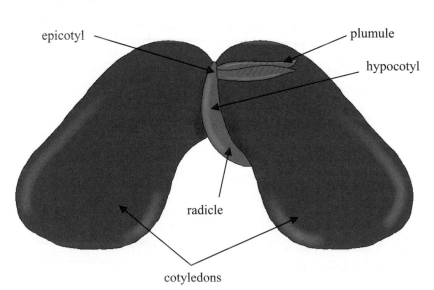

This is a drawing of the inside of a bean seed. The insides of other seeds can look different from this, but it is a good example.

Inside the Seed

The **cotyledons** are the biggest part of this embryo. They have a special purpose. They provide food for the embryo once the seed opens and the embryo starts growing into a plant. To grow, the embryo needs food, and it gets that food from the cotyledons until it can start making food for itself. You will learn about how a plant makes food for itself later. It is important for you to understand that you are looking at what is called a "mature seed." That means the seed can sprout as soon as it gets the water, warmth, and air that it needs. When the seed is attached to its mother plant (remember the hilum, where it attaches to its mother?), it is not yet mature.

What's the difference between a mature seed and an immature seed? In bean seeds, one big difference is the cotyledons. When the seed is immature, its cotyledons are small, and it has an **endosperm** (en' doh spurm). The endosperm is food for the embryo, but the embryo cannot eat it. To help the embryo eat the food, the cotyledons absorb the endosperm. This causes the cotyledons to grow into the biggest part of the embryo. When the seed finally opens and the embryo begins to grow, the cotyledons give it the food that they have absorbed.

Now remember, God made a lot of different kinds of seeds. Not all of them look like bean seeds. In some seeds, the cotyledons do not absorb the endosperm right away. Instead, they start to absorb the endosperm after the seed has opened. Then, they pass the food immediately to the embryo. In those kinds of seeds, the cotyledons are much smaller than in the seed that that you have been looking at, and the endosperm is there as a separate part of the seed.

The **radicle** is the embryo's root. It grows into the plant's root. When the radicle grows, it makes tiny little hairs. Those hairs are not hairs like you and I have; they are little fibers that go searching for water and nutrients. When they find these things, they absorb them and send them to the rest of the plant. You will do an experiment in a moment where you will get to watch the radicle grow and see these tiny little hairs.

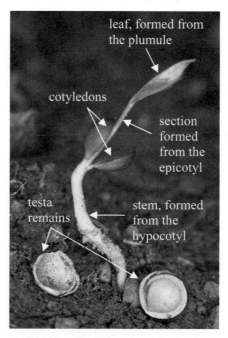

This is a picture of a plant sprouting.

The **hypocotyl** will become the stem. It will elongate (that means grow longer) and go searching for light if none is present. If light is present, it doesn't have to grow as long, so it will grow thicker. If no light is present, it will elongate further, hoping that by growing longer, it will reach light.

The **epicotyl** is the top of the embryo. It holds the **plumule**, which will become the first true leaves of the plant. Why do I say "true leaves?" Well, when the embryo begins to grow, the cotyledons actually look like leaves as well. They are not as green as the true leaves, but they look very similar to leaves. Because of this, some call the cotyledons the first leaves of the plant. However, they are not true leaves. **Plumule** is a Latin word that means **feather**. The plumule of your bean seed kind of looks like feathers, doesn't it?

Not all epicotyls have a plumule (leaves that have already developed). Most embryos do not have their true leaves when they are an embryo, but the bean embryo does. Have you ever seen a baby born with teeth? It doesn't happen often, but when it does, it's a big surprise. Usually the teeth don't grow in until a lot later. Well, that is what it's like for the bean plant. It already has its first true leaves, even though most plant embryos do not.

Since the bean plant starts out with its true leaves already developed, that gives it a head start on growing. After all, the leaves are a vital part of the plant. They actually make food for the plant. Why would God design one kind of seed to have a head start on growing? Most likely, it is because beans have a lot of protein. Protein is a very important nutrient that we must eat to stay healthy.

In Ezekial 4:8-13, we read that God told the prophet named Ezekiel to lie on the ground and eat only a certain kind of bread every day for more than a year. That bread was made with beans and other ingredients, and it provided all the protein he needed to live during that whole time. This shows us that beans are a good source of protein. God made beans so that they grow easily. They can grow in the coldest places and even with only a little water and light. It's not by accident that beans are easy to grow and that they are so healthy for us. God designed it that way to take care of us in difficult times of drought. In this way, God shows us His love and care with the simple little bean seed.

Beans are important seeds to have. If our food was ever difficult to get, but we had bean seeds, we could grow them and nourish our family. You may want to begin a seed collection. If you do, be sure to collect bean seeds!

Tell someone everything you can remember about the insides of a seed.

Germination

When water surrounds the seed, the testa loosens, just as you saw in the seed that you had been soaking. Water then gets inside the seed, and the embryo wakes up! This starts a process called **germination** (jur' muh nay' shun).

The radicle is the first thing to push its way out of the seed. After that, the hypocotyl and epicotyl poke out. They must go straight up through the dirt and break through the surface of the soil.

Now remember, the hypocotyl becomes the stem, and the epicotyl holds what will become the first true leaves of the plant (the plumule). In between the epicotyl and plumule, you will find the cotyledons. They come out of the soil with the plant, looking a lot like leaves. We often call them **seed leaves**. It's truly amazing that the cotyledons inside the seed transform so quickly into what look like leaves! The drawing below shows you how this process happens.

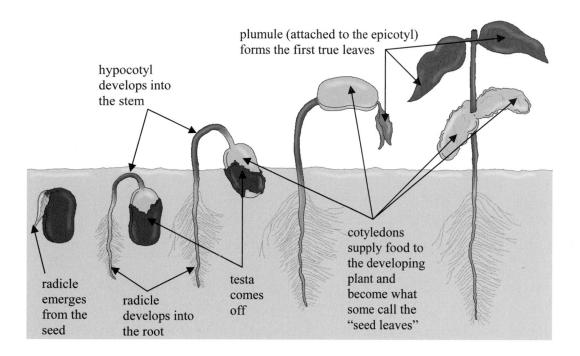

plumule (attached to the epicotyl) forms the first true leaves

hypocotyl develops into the stem

radicle emerges from the seed

radicle develops into the root

testa comes off

cotyledons supply food to the developing plant and become what some call the "seed leaves"

Do you remember what a seed needs to germinate? It needs warmth, air, and water. Do you remember that it doesn't need soil? Soil is filled with chemicals that the growing plant will need to stay healthy, so why doesn't the embryo need soil when it begins to germinate? Remember that all the nutrition it will need for several days is packed within the seed's endosperm. In some seeds, like your bean seed, the cotyledons absorb the endosperm. That means the cotyledons have all of the nutrition that the baby plant will need for several days. In other seeds, the cotyledons just absorb the endosperm as the baby plant needs the nutrition. Either way, all of the nutrition that the baby plant needs starts in the endosperm and ends up going through the cotyledons to the baby plant.

Can you guess what kind of food the endosperm is filled with? What is your very favorite thing to eat? Ice cream? Cake? Cookies? Whatever it is, it just might have some sugar in it. Well, guess what? The endosperm also has sugar in it! It has other nutrients that the plant needs as well, but it definitely has sugar. This is not the same kind of sugar you enjoy eating, but it is still sugar. Plants love sugar! They love sugar even more than you, because they cannot live without sugar. It is their food. It is so important to plants that God has designed them to make it themselves inside their leaves. What if you made sugar inside yourself that you could eat all day long?

Since God created plants to make their own food, they don't eat other plants to survive the way we do. They also don't eat animals to survive the way we do. We (and most of the creatures in creation) depend on other living things to survive. We consume other parts of God's creation to live, so we are called **consumers**. Plants produce their own food, so they are called **producers**.

What Do You Remember?

Describe germination. What is the top part of the embryo called? What are the feather-like leaves on the embryo called? What is the embryo's root called? What is the nutrition within the seed called before it gets absorbed by the cotyledons? What is the testa? Explain how the testa comes off for germination. What is a producer? What is a consumer? Are plants producers or consumers? Are people producers or consumers?

Notebook Activities

Create a page for this lesson in your notebook. Make an illustration of the different parts of a seed. Use your seed as an example. Label the parts on your illustration. Place your illustration in your notebook.

Older Students: Write down all that you remember about seeds in your notebook.

Younger Students: Tell your parent / teacher all that you remember about seeds so that she can write it down in your notebook.

Design a Coat

Do you remember what a seed coat is called? It's called a testa. We learned that there are many different colors and types of seed coats. I would like for you to design a special seed. Make the seed coat the color and pattern you would like to have if you were a seed. What kind of plant would your seed produce? Where would it grow? What would you name it? Put your drawing in your notebook.

Make a Germination Animation

Have you ever made a flip book? It is simply a notepad with pictures drawn in the bottom corner. The pictures show the same thing in changing positions or with changing features. If you position your hand so that it can flip through the book quickly, showing the pictures one after another at a very fast pace, it looks like your picture is moving. This is a simple version of how they make animated movies. In this activity, you are going to make a flip book of a seed germinating.

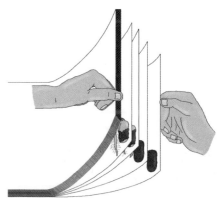

You will need:

- A pencil
- A pad of paper (You can staple pieces of paper together to make one if you don't have one.)

1. Start with the page at the bottom of the pad. Near the bottom of that page, draw the seed.
2. On the next page up, draw the same size seed at the same position, but then draw the radicle beginning to peek through.
3. On the next page, draw the radicle longer, but keep the seed in the same place.
4. On the next few pages, continue to draw the radicle longer, but also draw the epicotyl coming out.
5. In each successive picture, draw the seedling getting bigger and bigger, going through each of the stages drawn in the illustration on page 27.
6. Once you have finished, hold the pad down so that the bottom page (the one with just the seed drawn on it) is showing, but the other pages are curled up above it.
7. Let the pages fall down one at a time. As you watch, it will look like the seed is growing into a seedling right before your eyes!

Project
Germination

You will grow some seeds inside plastic bags so that you can watch their development and make a guess about which ones will grow best. You will write down all that you are going to do for this experiment and make a good guess about what you think is going to happen on the special science experiment sheet provided at the beginning of this book. It is called the *Scientific Speculation Sheet*. To speculate means to make guesses about something. You will use a sheet like that for many of the experiments that you do in this book.

You will need:

- Three plastic Ziploc® bags
- Three paper towels
- Three or more turnip seeds (or bean seeds)
- Tape
- A ruler (It should read centimeters.)
- A Scientific Speculation Sheet (found at beginning of book)

1. Wet three paper towels with water and place one inside each of the plastic bags.
2. Place a seed in each plastic bag. If you have more than three seeds, you can put more than one seed in each plastic bag. Zip each bag closed once you have put the seed or seeds in it.
3. Tape the first bag to a window that receives sunlight. Make sure your seed faces the window.
4. Place the second bag in your refrigerator.
5. Place the third bag in a dark closet that no one usually opens and never gets any light.
6. On your Scientific Speculation Sheet, write down your experiment and your guess about what will happen to each seed. For example, guess whether or not each seed will germinate, and guess which one will grow fastest and which one will grow slowest. This is called a **hypothesis** (hi pahth' uh sis).
7. Make a Seed Growth Chart for each bag. In other words, you will have one Seed Growth Chart for the seed that is in the bag taped to the window, another Seed Growth Chart for the seed in the dark closet, and another for the seed in the refrigerator. A sample Seed Growth Chart is given below.
8. To fill out each chart, use the ruler to measure the length of the plant (not the seed) each day. Put a dot in the square that marks the day you are making the measurement and the measurement that you made. For example, today is Day 1. Your seed has not grown at all today, so put a dot in the square that has "Day 1" on the bottom and "0 cm" to the left. Tomorrow will be Day 2. If any of the seedlings have sprouted, measure their lengths. Suppose that one seedling is 2 cm long by then. If that's the case, put a dot in the square that has "Day 2" below it and "2 cm" to its left.

Seed Growth Chart

	Day 1	Day 2	Day 3	Day 4	Day 5	Day 6	Day 7	Day 8	Day 9	Day 10	Day 11	Day 12
6 cm												
5 cm												
4 cm												
3 cm												
2 cm												
1 cm												
0 cm												

9. At the end of twelve days, compare the Seed Growth Charts. The seed that has dots highest on the chart the soonest is the one that grew the fastest. Which one was that? Was your hypothesis correct?

Monocotyledons and Dicotyledons

Do you remember from Lesson 1 that we classify seed-making plants into angiosperms and gymnosperms? Those are two different phyla. Botanists further classify the angiosperms into two classes based on the number of cotyledons the seed has: **monocots** and **dicots**. **Di** means **two**. This tells us that dicots have two cotyledons. **Mono** means **one**. There is only one cotyledon in a monocot seed. Based on what you saw in your bean seed, is the bean plant a monocot or a dicot? Since it has two cotyledons, it is a dicot!

Why is it important to determine whether or not a plant is a monocot or dicot? Believe it or not, monocot plants look different from dicot plants. Look, for example, at the two photographs below.

Corn is a monocot. Notice the veins the leaves. They do not branch at all. They run straight up and down.

The primrose plant is a dicot. Notice how the veins in the leaves branch out from a center vein.

Monocot leaves have veins going upwards to the top of the leaf, not branching out from a thick, center midrib vein. Next time you are looking at the leaf of a plant, look at the veins. If the veins never branch out but instead just form lines that run up and down the leaf, the plant is a monocot. If the veins branch out from a vein running down the middle of the leaf, the plant is a dicot.

Another difference between monocots and dicots can be seen if you look at their flowers. Remember, angiosperms are flowering plants, so all monocots and dicots make flowers. However, their flowers are usually a bit different. Monocot flowers usually have petals in multiples of three. Can you count by threes? Three, six, nine. If you count the petals on a flower and find that there are three, six, or nine petals, then the plant is most likely a monocot. On the other hand, dicots usually have flowers that have petals in multiples of four or five. In other words, dicot flowers might have four petals or eight petals. They might also have five petals or ten petals. Look at the photographs on the next page to see what I mean.

The daffodil is a monocot. Notice that it has six petals around the flower.

The marigold is a dicot. Notice that it has five petals around the flower.

It is useful for you to know how to identify whether or not a plant is a monocot or a dicot. The easiest way, of course, is to open up the plant's seed and count the number of cotyledons. If there is one, the plant is a monocot. If there are two, the plant is a dicot. If you don't have seeds handy, however, looking at the leaves or the flowers will usually do the trick.

Explain to someone else the difference between monocots and dicots. Make sure you describe the differences between the seeds, leaves, and flowers.

Notebook Activities
Identify Plants

Are these plants monocots or dicots? Look at the leaves and flowers to help you decide.

A   B   C   D

The correct answers for this activity can be found in the "Answers to the Narrative Questions" section near the end of the book.

Nature Walk in a Yard

Today you will take your notebook, paper, and some colored pencils outside on a search for monocots and dicots. Monocots are the most difficult to find in nature, especially in winter. Look for leaves that have vertical (going up and down) veins that travel the length of the leaf or flowers that have petals in multiples of three. I will give you a hint on how to find at least one monocot. Get down on your knees on any lawn. Look carefully at the blades of grass. Notice the veins. Draw the monocots you find and label them in your notebook. Do the same thing for dicots. After you have drawn a picture of a monocot or dicot, label your drawing so others will know why the plant you drew is a monocot or a dicot.

Optional Winter Activity

If you cannot go outside today, put it off for a while and do the following project. You may want to do this activity even if you are able to go out.

Go through old magazines from which you have permission to cut out pictures. If none are available, you can use the internet to find botanical gardens or flower shops. When you come across a picture of a plant, leaf or flower, try to identify whether it is a monocot or dicot. Cut out or print the picture and glue it onto a piece of paper. Label it as a monocot or a dicot. Be certain to write down why you think it is a monocot or dicot. Place your completed, labeled pictures in your notebook.

Project
Seed Collecting

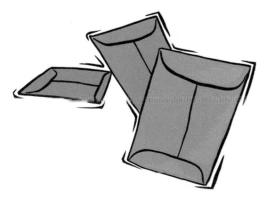

This is a good time to begin a seed collection. Every time you eat a piece of fruit, save the seeds and let them dry out. When they are dry, place them in tiny envelopes, such as coin envelopes. You can also make envelopes with the pattern on the next page. Seal them up and put them in a special place. If you have page protectors with small pouches designed for sports card collections, you can place your seed envelopes in those pouches. Label your seeds. They will keep for a long time!

Seed Collection Envelope Pattern

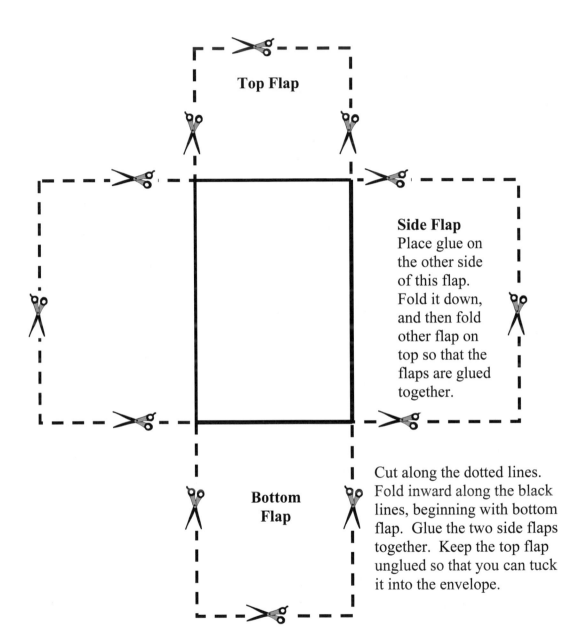

Top Flap

Side Flap
Place glue on
the other side
of this flap.
Fold it down,
and then fold
other flap on
top so that the
flaps are glued
together.

**Bottom
Flap**

Cut along the dotted lines.
Fold inward along the black
lines, beginning with bottom
flap. Glue the two side flaps
together. Keep the top flap
unglued so that you can tuck
it into the envelope.

Lesson 3
Flowers

Note to the teacher: For this lesson, you will need one fresh flower, paper, and either tape or glue. The flower must **not** be a composite flower (like a chrysanthemum or sunflower), but a composite flower would be excellent for hands-on observation. For information about this, read the "Flower Families" section of this lesson. Flower shops or the flower section of your grocery store might give you their discards, if you ask.

Do you remember what angiosperms are? They are plants that make flowers. A lot of plants on God's glorious earth are angiosperms. God had a special use for these kinds of plants, and He applied an amazing amount of creativity and care in designing each of them.

What use did God design for angiosperms? Well, let's try, for just a moment, to imagine life without angiosperms. What would our lives look like? What would the world look like? Without angiosperms, the world would be a *very* different place! There would be no beans to eat. Do you remember how important beans are to people's health? Well, bean plants make flowers, so they are angiosperms. There would also be no fruits, and many of the vegetables we eat would not exist, either. But that's not all! Without angiosperms, we would have no wheat, no rice, and no oats. That means no bread, cereal, or oatmeal.

Angiosperms are a beautiful and necessary part of God's glorious creation!

These things keep us healthy. Without angiosperms, then, our health would suffer. Wait a minute. Meat does not come from angiosperms, so even if there were no angiosperms, we could still eat meat, couldn't we? Well, most of the meat that we eat (except for fish) comes from animals that eat grass, wheat, corn, and other plants. These animals are called **herbivores** (ur' bih vors), because they eat only plants. Most of the plants that they eat are angiosperms. Without angiosperms, these herbivores would probably all die, leaving us with only fish to eat. Think also about animals like lions and tigers. These animals eat only meat and are called **carnivores** (kar' nih vors). Without herbivores, carnivores could not survive, because the meat that they eat comes mostly from herbivores. If God allowed the earth to quit producing angiosperms, where would we all be? We would probably all be fishing, because fish would be about the only thing to eat!

Without angiosperms, we would not have cotton plants to make our clothes and sheets. We couldn't snuggle up on our nice warm bed at night, because there wouldn't be any cuddly comforter or sheets on it. A lot of our clothing comes from cotton and other fabrics made from angiosperms or from animals that must eat angiosperms to survive. Without angiosperms, then, we might not even have clothes to wear!

If there were no flowers, there would be no nectar for bees, because angiosperms make nectar and put it in their flowers. This means there would be no honey! Without angiosperms, there would be no sugar cane plants to give us sugar and fill our birthday parties with cakes and cookies. There would be no maple trees for the sweet maple syrup that drips on our pancakes. In fact, no angiosperms would also mean no pancakes! The world without angiosperms is already sounding a lot less sweet, isn't it?

Praise God for angiosperms! Not only do they provide our lives with essential things we need to survive on this earth, they are also beautiful to behold. The Lord knew we would need what angiosperms make, and He planned out their purposes before He made man. Do you realize that angiosperms were on the earth on the third day of creation?

The angiosperms provide us with a lot of what we need, but did God have to make the flowering plants so lovely for our eyes to behold? No. The Lord did not have to make the grass on our lawns such a beautiful, calming green, nor the trees so majestic and tall against the sky, nor the flowers in spring so full of splendor and beauty. The Lord could have just as easily made all the trees filled with leaves of a dull gray color, the grass the same dull gray, and the flowers all the same dreary, uninteresting gray. The Lord did not have to make all the amazing colors: pinks, blues, purples, yellows, oranges, and reds that we see. All these beautiful colors are a feast to our eyes and a gift from the Lord.

The beauty of flowers is a gift from God.

Why do you think God made the world so much more lovely and interesting than He had to?
Well, have you ever drawn a picture that took you a long time? Did you put a lot of thought and

details in the picture? If so, then you have gotten a
tiny glimpse of how God feels about His world and
all He made. He took great care and put much
thought into everything He made. The beauty that
God placed in the world tells us about the character
of God. We know that He cares about us and
wanted to make the world a lovely place for us to
live. When you enjoy the sunset, the flowers, the
trees, and a nice cool breeze, remember that they
are gifts from God, and thank Him in your heart.

The things we draw or work on are special to us while we are focused on them. Sadly, we
easily forget about the things we have made or done, always moving on to the next thing. Thankfully,
God never does that. He is still focusing on His creation. He is diligently working on the details of
every single thing that happens on this earth, though he formed it long ago. He sees every caterpillar
egg that hatches, every hair on your head, and every tear in your eye. He loves you so much and wants
the best for you. He is always making sure that things work out according to His perfect plan for your
life. All of nature must obey Him, and He is in control of all things.

Even the Flowers Obey

Just like all things, flowers obey God's plan and design for
them. God's purpose in creating them was not only for our
pleasure, but they actually have a very grand purpose for being.
The flower's job is to make babies! Do you remember where all
baby plants begin? They begin as an embryo in a seed. All
flowers make seeds, even the tiniest ones. That is their God-given
purpose in life.

Making Seeds

All flowers make seeds. Notice the seeds
forming in this sunflower.

How flowers make seeds is simply another miracle of God.
God developed flowers in such a special way, and I want you to
learn more about them. To do this, we will take apart a flower. When we take something apart to
study it, we say we are **dissecting** (die sekt' ing) it. As you dissect a flower, you will be learning about
flower **anatomy**. Anatomy simply means the study of the different parts of a living thing. The
anatomy of the flower will teach you about how flowers make seeds.

Flower Dissection

You will need:

♦ A flower (This cannot be a composite flower. It must have visible stamens and a carpel, such as the flower pictured on page 39.)

♦ A piece of paper

♦ Glue or tape

♦ An adult with a knife

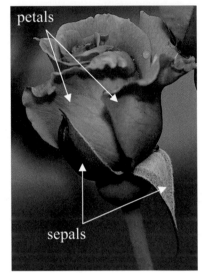

1. Study your flower for a moment.

2. Turn your flower upside down. On most flowers you will see green leaf-like "points" under the petals. Does your flower have them? If not, they may have fallen off. They are called **sepals** (see' puls). Look at the sepals on the rose pictured to the right. The sepals work together to cover and protect the developing flower. Before the flower blooms, it is a bud. The bud is covered by the sepals, which are usually green. Then, as the bud opens, the sepals separate, ending up under the flower. Because the sepals are no longer needed after the flower blooms, they often fall off. On certain flowers, however, the sepals stay attached to the base of the flower, just above the stem. All of the sepals together are called the **calyx** (kal' ix) of the flower.

3. Using your fingers, carefully pull each sepal off your flower. Once you have gotten all of the sepals of the calyx, lay them flat on a piece of paper and secure them with tape or glue. Using glue will sometimes keep the sepals from losing their green color. Label them "sepals" and "calyx."

4. Using your fingers, carefully begin removing the petals one by one. Be certain to remove each entire petal, and not just the uppermost part. The petal reaches all the way down to the top of the stem. Once again, glue them onto paper. All of the petals together are called the **corolla** (kor oh' luh). When you have removed all of the petals of the corolla and glued them on paper, label them "petals" and "corolla."

5. Did you get any slimy stuff on you as you removed the corolla? That slimy stuff is the **nectar** (nek' tur), which is kept at the base of each petal. Birds, bees, butterflies, and many insects love this sweet juice, which is why you see them flying around flowers.

6. What you now have left are the most interesting parts of your flower! What you are probably looking at right now are the boy and girl parts of the flowers. Yes, indeed! Almost all flowers have male and female parts within them. These parts aren't male and female the way you and I are male and female, but they are similar enough that botanists have named them that way. Remember, the same hand that made you and me also made the flowers. Of course, then, all that He made would be somewhat similar. The male part of a flower makes the female part of a flower pregnant so that it can make seeds. Let's learn more about this exciting seed making business. First, however, I want to review what you have learned so far.

What Do You Remember?

What is so special about angiosperms? What is the purpose of a flower? What is the job of the sepal? What are all of the sepals together called? Explain what the corolla is. Now let's continue on with our dissection.

7. The next things you see on your flower are the male parts. The male parts of the flower are the little stalks, or poles, that all look basically the same. Each of these little stalks is called a **stamen** (stay' men). It's easy to remember because males are men, and "sta**men**" has the word "**men**" in it. The stamen's job is to make pollen. There should be one stalk that looks different from the stamen. That is the female part of the plant. Can you recognize the stamens in your flower? There may be a lot more than what is pictured in the flower on the right.

8. Each stamen has a pole called the **filament** (fill' uh ment). Sometimes the pole is tiny; sometimes it is very long. Sometimes it is attached to a center portion of the flower; sometimes it simply surrounds the center structure of the flower. At the top of every filament is an enlarged part covered with pollen called the **anther** (an' thur). Can you find the anther and filament on one of the stamens in your flower?

9. Remove an anther from one of the stamens. Be careful not to remove the female part of the flower. We will learn about the female part in a moment. If you have a magnifying glass, study the anther with it. Shake a bit of the dust off, if it is still there. Place it on your paper and glue it down. Label it "anther." Anthers are usually covered with thousands of pollen grains, so small that, all together, they make a fine dust. The dust is actually thousands of grains of pollen. Inside each pollen grain are two little sperms. Do you remember what a sperm is? We learned from the word angiosperm that sperm means seed. Pollen, then, is a kind of seed! In fact, it is really about half of a seed. When pollen reaches the female part of a flower, it will dig into the female part until it finds a tiny egg there. It will then join with that egg to make a seed. Isn't that simply astonishing?

10. Remove the rest of the stamens from your flower and place them on your paper. Label the filaments and anthers.

Before we go on to study the female part of the flower, explain in your own words what you have learned about the male part of the flower. Make sure you explain what the male part of the flower is called, what its parts are called, and what its parts do.

11. The only thing you should have left of your flower now is the female part and the stem. The female part of the flower is called the **carpel** (car' pul), and it is attached to the center of the flower. There is usually only one carpel per flower, but sometimes there are more. How many carpels does your flower have? Most carpels are long and thin, but some are short and fat. Look at the flowers below and notice the different shapes that carpels come in. Is your carpel like any of these? Carpel shapes, sizes, and colors are some of the most interesting things to study. God truly used marvelous and imaginative design with all the unusual carpel shapes. You would be simply amazed at all the distinct kinds of carpels there are in this world.

12. At the top of the carpel is a sticky head called the **stigma**. The stigma is sticky because it is designed to catch any pollen that touches it. Remember that the pollen meets with the egg down inside the carpel to make seeds. That's why the stigma wants to catch pollen.

13. The stigma is on top of a long tube, called the **style**. This is the tube that the pollen goes down to get to the egg.

14. Down at the bottom of the style, the very bottom part of the carpel, is the flower's **ovary** (oh' vuh ree). Each ovary contains little tiny egg-shaped structures called **ovules** (oh' vyools).

15. Now that you have removed everything from your flower except the carpel, it is time to dissect the carpel to see if there are ovules inside. Using a knife is very dangerous; please have a grown up slice your carpel in half vertically, as shown in the drawing on the right.

16. Inside the ovary of your carpel, you might see tiny little things that look like eggs. Those are the ovules. The ovules contain the eggs, which are too small for you to see. Do you remember when I told you that pollen is like half of a seed? Well, the eggs inside the ovules are the other half! When the pollen digs down through the style and into the ovary, it will find an ovule and meet up with one of the eggs. When the two join, the plant has everything it needs to make a seed. Isn't that remarkable?

17. Attach the carpel to paper and label its parts. When the glue on your papers dries, you can place the pages that contain your dissected flower into your notebook.

To help you remember all of the parts of a flower, I have included a drawing below. Now that you have seen a real flower and touched all of its parts, you should be able to understand this drawing.

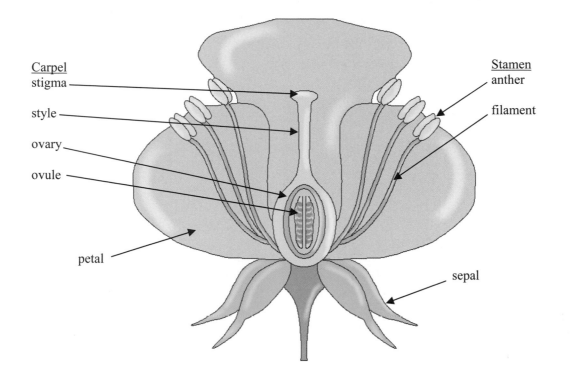

Carpel
stigma
style
ovary
ovule
petal

Stamen
anther
filament

sepal

Tell someone about all the parts of the flower that you have studied. Try to do it without looking at this book or your notebook. Be sure to tell the person where the eggs and pollen are and how the pollen gets to the eggs. ✶

Flower Families

Angiosperms have been grouped into families by botanists. There are so many angiosperms that botanists list more than 300 such families! How similar are the plants in a single family? Well, let's think about the rose family. The Latin name for this family is "Rosaceae" (rohs' uh see' uh). The rose family includes roses (like the one pictured on page 38), but it also includes flowers that grow on some trees, such as the cherry tree flowers pictured on the right. Why are cherry trees grouped in the same family as roses? It's because their flowers have very similar features. Sure, there are a lot of differences between a rose bush and a cherry tree, but they have enough in common to put them into the same family.

The cherry tree is a part of the rose family, Rosaceae.

Since there are so many families of angiosperms, I cannot talk about them all. However, I do want to spend some time on a few very interesting flower families. One is the sunflower family, whose Latin name is "Asteraceae" (as' tur uh see' uh). This family is interesting because its members produce **composite flowers**. Some composite flowers you may be familiar with are sunflowers, chrysanthemums (or mums), daisies, and asters. Look at each of the flowers pictured below and describe something you see that is similar about them all.

Daisy   Sunflowers   Aster

Can you see stamens and carpels in these flowers? No. Instead, the center of the flower is a mass of tiny structures. That makes these flowers composite flowers. Composite flowers are fabulously complex. They are nothing like any other flower we have studied so far. You see, they are not just one flower, but a mass of hundreds of flowers on one stalk! Each composite flower has a special thick mass in the center. That thick mass is actually a group of tiny flowers that are growing upon a round, flat disk. What at first seems to be a single large flower is actually a composite, or combination, of many smaller flowers. Each tiny flower in the center has its own tiny stamens and carpel, with itty bitty ovules deep within. Even the things that look like petals are, in fact, individual flowers! They are called **ray flowers**, because they surround the central disk like the rays of the sun.

If you can find a dandelion from outside, look closely at it, and you will see that there are hundreds of little flowers growing on the flower's disk. Each of these little flowers produces just one seed. Each of these teeny, tiny flowers has 5 itty-bitty petals fused together. Look closely at the big "petals" that ring the outside of the flower head. Those are the ray flowers. Now wouldn't you agree that the composite flower is an interesting creation?

The dandelion is a composite flower. Notice the tiny, individual stalks. Each is an individual flower!

Carnivorous Plants

Do you remember what a carnivore is? It's an animal that eats meat. The root word **carn** is a Latin word meaning **meat**. Can you think of an animal that eats meat? Animals that eat grass are herbivores. Most carnivores eat herbivores. We also use the word **carnivorous** to describe these animals.

This may sound a little scary at first, but there are actually plants that are carnivorous as well. Don't worry; none of them could or would ever eat you. Most of these plants are tiny, only a few inches high, and only a few are big enough to ingest a small frog. Though these plants act just like any other angiosperm in every other way, they are different because they are able to absorb certain nutrients from animals.

Carnivorous plants actually have special mechanisms inside them that cause visiting insects and sometimes small amphibians (like frogs) to get stuck inside of them. Sometimes it's a trap, and sometimes it's a sticky goo that the animal gets stuck in. Then, they digest these unfortunate visitors so that that they can get an important nutrient called nitrogen. All plants need nitrogen, and they are usually able to get plenty of it from the soil. Carnivorous plants, however, are able to live in poor soil or swamp areas where nitrogen is not easily absorbed. God created them to make up for the lack of nitrogen in the soil by getting it from small animals in the area. That was a very imaginative idea, wasn't it? There are several families of carnivorous plants. Let's look at some common ones.

The Venus Flytrap Family

The **Venus flytrap** family is probably the most famous family of carnivorous plants. The first Venus flytrap was discovered in North America on the coast of North and South Carolina, where it grows wild near the Cape Fear River. You can easily buy these plants today to keep in your home, as they are found in plant stores all over the country.

If you look for a Venus flytrap in the store, don't look for anything big. The Venus flytrap is a small plant, with tiny little leaves. Its small clam-shaped leaves are lined with bristles on each edge and put out a sweet aroma to attract insects. Inside the leaves, there are tiny, almost microscopic, hairs that respond to touch by snapping the leaf shut. If one hair is touched, such as with a stick, it will remain open, but if two hairs are touched (one after the other), the trap is triggered, and the leaves snap shut. The fact that the leaf requires two hairs to be touched protects the plant from snapping shut when a non-living thing touches it. Only living things move around

The poor fly in this photo is about to be trapped and digested by the Venus flytrap.

enough to cause two hairs to be touched one after another. The Venus flytrap consumes ants, flies, moths, beetles, grasshoppers, and worms. People have tried to give their Venus flytrap pieces of hamburger, but that is not good for the plant. The plant is designed to use entire animals, not just the meat from the animal.

After it traps the insect with a sweet smelling, tiny leaf, the Venus flytrap takes about three days to digest the entire thing. After that, the leaf will open up again, ready for a new creature to happen upon it. Now it is important to understand that the Venus flytrap *does not eat insects for food*. Like all plants, the Venus flytrap makes its own food to eat. The Venus flytrap, like all carnivorous plants, uses the animals it digests as a source of **nitrogen**, which you can think of as a vitamin for the plant. Do you take vitamins? They are not your food, but they help to keep you healthy, right? Well, plants need vitamins, too, and the Venus flytrap gets some of its vitamins from the insects that it digests.

The Bladderwort Family

A **bladderwort** is a carnivorous plant that looks perfectly normal from above. It grows small, beautiful flowers on its long, bare stems. If you look down below (where roots belong), however, you will find multiple tiny traps that hang in the water. These traps are actually tiny sacs that act like vacuums, sucking in tiny water critters. As you probably guessed, these plants grow in swampy, wet areas. Their little sacs are called bladders. That is why we call the plant a bladderwort. Their bladder-like traps are tiny, less than an inch small. They are sometimes as small as a pinhead.

The bladderwort looks like any other flower, but has a secret in its roots.

Within the bladder, a trapdoor is held closed by a thin film of a glue-like substance that blocks the entrance. Special trigger hairs near the lower edge of the trapdoor cause it to open when a creature hits

This drawing illustrates the bladders on the roots of the bladderwort.

against them. Immediately, in less than a second, the creature is sucked inside the bladder like a vacuum cleaner sucks in dirt from the carpet. After that, little glands inside the bladder release chemicals that digest all the soft parts of the creature. Bladderworts trap and eat water fleas, worms, and small insects. The larger bladderworts can even catch tiny fish!

Bladderworts live in nearly every country of the world. They prefer areas that lack enough of the "vitamins" that plants need. Since they get their "vitamins" from the creatures they catch, they can live in such places, while non-carnivorous plants find it much harder to live in those same places.

The Pitcher Plant Family

Perhaps the most frightening member of the carnivorous plant group is the **pitcher plant**. It is frightening because it is known to consume larger animals. It's a plant that develops vase-like tubes that grow straight up from its grass-like stems. There are many different species.   One species has a hood-like cover over the vase; a very common American species looks very much like a flower vase.

Inside the vase is a cup of sweet-smelling nectar that attracts bugs and small animals to its lip. When the animal tries to get a little closer for a delicious sip, it slides down the extremely slippery sides of the vase and finds itself trapped inside. Why can't it just climb out? After all, a bug can crawl up almost anything. Well, it is because there are small prickles pointing down into the base of the cup that continually poke the creature when it attempts to climb. In addition, the vase is filled with rainwater. After struggling for several minutes, the creature drowns, and within 3 hours, it is completely consumed by the pitcher plant. In the end, there is nothing left of the little creature but the exoskeleton (hard, shell-like body of the insect) or bones. These bones and exoskeletons just stay there at the bottom of the vase.

Notice how this pitcher plant looks like a vase with a little "hood" over the opening.

Though the pitcher plant was created to consume insects, some birds, frogs, and rodents have been known to fall into the vase and be consumed by the plant. It is very difficult for the plant to consume such large animals, and it often weakens the plant. After all, it is designed to get the nitrogen it needs from tiny insects. It really would rather not have to digest big animals. However, if a big animal falls in the vase, there is no way for the pitcher plant to get rid of it, so the pitcher plant is forced to digest it.

The Sundew Family

Sundews are an amazing creation of God. These tiny, spiny, flowering plants grow to be about five inches tall. That is probably as tall as your mom's hand. They are found everywhere in the world except Antarctica. The flowers come in many colors. On the ends of each flower stalk are tentacles that ooze wonderful-smelling, sticky goo. This goo oozes down the plant, and it smells so wonderful that it attracts sugar-loving creatures day and night. Of course, this sweet-smelling goo is actually a trap. It is made of chemicals that not only ensnare insects but also digest them so that the plant can get its "vitamins" from the insect.

Here is how it works. A fly, butterfly, or other nectar-loving insect will detect the sweet smell of the liquid that oozes from the plant. Landing on the colorful tip, the insect will immediately be stuck. The plant has cells that send messages to the plant when an insect arrives. This tells the plant to make more goo in the area where the insect is. The plant then produces a massive amount of goo from the nearby tentacles. The goo completely surrounds the insect. Then, the sundew plant will slowly wrap its tentacles around the insect, absorbing its nutrients. The sundew will consume the entire insect except the exoskeleton. Once the plant is done with its job, it opens up its tentacles and drops the exoskeleton to the ground.

Sundews are pretty, but for insects, they are very dangerous!

Like all carnivorous plants, sundews are marvels of engineering! They produce their own "bait" to attract insects; they have a way of detecting when an insect touches them; and they have a way of trapping the insect so that it cannot get away while it is being digested. Now remember, all of this is done so that carnivorous plants can live where it is difficult for other plants to live. God's creation is truly incredible!

What Do You Remember?

What is the nutrient that carnivorous plants use from the creatures they digest? How does a Venus flytrap keep from shutting its leaf when something other than an animal falls into its trap? Describe the bladderwort and how it traps its prey. Why is the pitcher plant the most frightening of the carnivorous plants? Explain why creatures trapped in the pitcher plant cannot escape it. Explain how sundews trap and digest animals.

Notebook Activities

Older Students: On a sheet of paper, draw a picture of a flower, including all of the major parts you learned about in this lesson (stamen, carpel, petals, and sepals). Label all of the parts of the drawing. You can use the drawing on page 41 as a guide. Put this in front of your flower dissection pages.

Younger Students: On a sheet of paper, draw your favorite flowers from this lesson. Put this page in front of your flower dissection pages.

All Students: On a sheet of paper, write down (or dictate to your parent so that she can write it down) the facts you found most interesting about the carnivorous plants that you studied. Draw at least one of the plants, explaining in detail how it traps the animals that it digests.

Nature Walk Activity

Take a nature walk with paper and colored pencils. Begin a search for flowers of all varieties. When you come to a flower, study it closely. Observe and make a sketch of the flower's carpel, stamens, petals, and sepals. Notice the carpel in particular. You will find great variety in the design of carpels as you search from flower to flower. Next to your sketch, make a sketch of the entire flower and plant, if there is room. If you know what kind of plant you are drawing, you may want to make note of that.

Make a separate notebook page for each flower you sketch. Place all of your completed drawings in your notebook. If flowers arc not in season at this time, plan a trip to a nursery or a botanical garden that has an indoor garden.

Projects
Build a Clay Model of a Flower

You will need:

- Construction paper (a bright color)
- Play-Doh®, clay, or salt dough (1 cup of flour, ¼ cup salt, ¼- ½ cup water)
- Cotton swabs (such as Q-tips®) or pipe cleaners
- Scissors

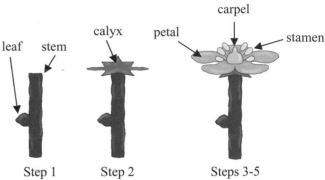

Instructions:

1. Roll your clay to make the stem of your flower. The thicker the stem, the better your flower will stay atop the stem. Add a leaf to the stem.
2. Use the clay to make a calyx (remember, that's all of the sepals together) on top of the stem.
3. Use the construction paper to make a corolla (remember, that's all of the petals together) on top of the calyx.
4. Use the clay to build a carpel. Look back at the different carpel designs in this book or make up a new carpel design. Make sure there is a bulge at the bottom to represent the ovary.
5. Use cut up cotton swabs or pipe cleaners to make stamen surrounding the carpel. If you are using pipe cleaners, put little lumps of clay on the ends to represent the anthers.

Preserve a Fresh Flower

You can preserve the color of a leaf or flower by completely surrounding it with borax in a covered container for about 2 weeks. When you retrieve the flower, it will be the same color it was when you placed it in the borax, but it will be dried out! The color will last a long time.

You will need:

- A fresh flower
- A box that can close
- Tape
- Borax

Instructions:

1. Pour a layer of borax into your box.
2. Place the flower in the box and cover it with the rest of the borax.
3. Close the box and tape it shut.
4. In two weeks, open it to remove your dried, preserved flower!

Lesson 4
Pollination

Note to the teacher: For this lesson, you will need a cotton swab (like a Q-tip®) and a couple of flowers, because you will be manually pollinating them. The flowers need to be attached to their plants, because you want the pollinated one to continue to develop. If you grew squash in your light hut, one flower can self pollinate, so you will only need one plant.

The way God designed a flower to make seeds is very fascinating. In order to make a seed, pollen must get from the anther to the stigma. In other words, pollen must get from the stamen to the carpel. How does it do that? "That's easy!" you say, "They are right next to each other." Although that is true, it doesn't help much. If pollen from a stamen goes to the carpel on the same flower, we call this **self-pollination**, because the flower is pollinating itself. Although some plants can make seeds through self-pollination, God designed most flowers so that they cannot self-pollinate. For most plants, pollen from one plant must get to the flower of a nearby plant of the same kind. In other words, the pollen on the stamen from the pear tree in my yard must get to the carpels on the pear tree in my neighbor's yard. But how does that happen?

Actually, there are at least two answers to this question. Wind can carry pollen from one plant to another, but that is not very efficient. After all, wind blows in many directions. Pollination from one plant to another will only happen if the wind is blowing just right. Fortunately, God has designed another way for pollen to travel between plants. Animals can help plants pollinate one another! Animals, especially bees and butterflies, accidentally carry the pollen from one flower to the next when they are looking for nectar. Remember from the previous lesson that plants make nectar and put it in their flowers. Birds, bees, butterflies, and other animals eat this sweet nectar, and they accidentally get pollen on their bodies. Then, when they move on to the next plant to get more nectar, they transfer pollen to the stigma of that plant's flowers.

This insect is helping to pollinate flowers.

Although I will talk about wind pollination and even self-pollination later on in this lesson, I want to concentrate on how animals help plants pollinate one another, because it is an incredibly fascinating process!

Animal Pollination

On the fifth day of creation, God created the birds, bees, bats, and butterflies (all flying creatures). On the same day, He also created the creatures that live in water, such as fish. Just two days after He created plants, He created the animals that would help them in pollination.

Do you realize that bees, butterflies, and certain other animals eat nectar in order to survive? The Lord made some animals and some plants dependent upon each other. Do you know what "dependent" means? It means needing something or someone. Are you dependent on anyone or anything? Most children are dependent on their parents, and we are all dependent on the mercy and grace of God. Even those who do not believe in God are still dependent on Him, even though they would never admit it.

The fact that some plants and animals are dependent on one another gives us evidence that God made the earth in 6 days that were each 24 hours in length. You see, some people think that God took longer than six, 24-hour days to create the earth. They believe that maybe each day mentioned in Genesis lasted

Hummingbirds eat the nectar found in flowers. The flower makes food for the hummingbird, and the hummingbird helps the flower spread its pollen.

thousands, millions, or even billions of years. However, it is unlikely that plants could have survived for long without animals to help them pollinate. After all, it would have been much harder for flowers to complete their special, God-given purpose of making new seeds without animals to help them

Like hummingbirds, butterflies feed on nectar, helping the flower spread its pollen.

pollinate. If the days in Genesis were really thousands, millions, or billions of years, the animals would not have appeared on earth for a long, long time after plants were created. Without the help of animals, plants would have a hard time making new seeds, and without a lot of new seeds, the plants would have died out. It makes sense, then, to believe that the days in Genesis are 24-hour days, because that way, plants would have only needed to wait for 48 hours before they could start making seeds.

So how do animals pollinate the flowers? Well, they must get their nectar from **nectaries** (nek' tuh rees) that are at the bottom of the flower. In order for animals to get to the nectar, they must pass by the stamens, which are topped with pollen. As they do this, they get pollen on their bodies. They must also pass by the carpel on their way to the nectar, and the sticky stigma on top of the carpel catches some of the pollen that they got on their bodies while they were at another flower. That way, pollen from one flower gets transferred to another flower.

Each flower has special colors, shapes, and smells to attract the animals that are designed by God to help the flower spread its pollen. Let's look at some of these animals to see how this works.

Bees

You probably already know that bees make honey. Why do they make honey? It is the food that they eat during the winter. When flowers are available, bees eat nectar and pollen. During the winter, however, they eat honey. What do bees make the honey out of? They make it out of nectar that they get from flowers! Not only do bees use nectar from flowers, they also use the pollen. They eat pollen as a source of protein, and they also mix it with honey to make what some call "bee bread."

Because they use both nectar and pollen, bees are always on the hunt for flowers. As a result, they are the most important pollinators of many flowers. If you see a bee, it is most likely either looking for a flower or on its way home from visiting a flower.

Some people keep bees to make honey. They keep them in bee boxes outside in their yard. The flowers that are in or near the bee keeper's yard get many little visitors each and every day of the spring, summer, and fall. These fortunate

Bee keepers have boxes in which bees can live. They collect and sell the honey made by these bees.

plants are sure to produce many new seeds, because the bees help them pollinate each other. Do you see a lot of bees when you go outside? If so, perhaps there is a bee keeper somewhere nearby.

Bees spend a lot of time on flowers.

Wait a minute. If bees spend a lot of time going from flower to flower, how does that help? What if the bee visits a rose, then hops over to a day lily, then flies to a pear tree blossom for a moment, and then heads home. The Bible says that each plant can only reproduce after its own kind (Gen 1:11-12). That means that the flowers can only be pollinated by flowers of the same kind. In other words, a rose carpel can only use pollen from the stamen of another rose. A day lily must have the pollen from another day lily to make day lily seeds. How does it happen that bees carry pollen of one flower to another flower of the same kind?

God, in His amazing wisdom, took all of this into account when He designed bees. Every day, each colony of bees decides what kind of flower to look for, and they all collect nectar and pollen from that one type of flower. They don't just fly around looking for any flower with pollen. Instead, they are on a mission to find one single kind of flower. This is truly a miracle! Have you ever seen a flowering plant simply covered with bees? They are probably all from the same colony, collecting the same kind of pollen and nectar for their food-making duties. This makes it easier for plants to get pollinated correctly, because a bee that

Bees from the same hive tend to look for the same flowers.

visits one flower on any given day was most likely just visiting a nearby flower of the same kind! God truly thought of everything when He designed the world!

Creation Confirmation

Did you know that some people actually believe that all of the animals and plants in creation just happened with no plan or design? These people, who are often called **evolutionists** (ev' uh loo' shun ists), believe that every plant and animal developed its special parts and features through a random process called **evolution**. They think that as plants and animals made new baby plants and animals, the baby plants and animals would have something new that their parents didn't have. If this new thing made it easier for the baby plants and animals to survive, when those babies grew up and had babies of their own, they would pass on this new thing to their babies. As time went on, evolutionists believe that these random new things kept "piling up" until the babies looked nothing like their great, great, great, great grandparents. In this way, a fish, for example, might have produced great, great, great, great grandchildren that were not fish at all, but were frogs instead. Evolutionists believe that all of the wonderful life forms that we see in creation today are the result of this random process. Bees give us evidence against this belief.

The very fact that bees look for one kind of flower instead of stopping at any flower they see is strong evidence against the idea of evolution. After all, the main idea behind evolution is that animals develop traits and habits that make it easiest for them to survive. The survival of a bee would be a lot easier if it could get nectar and pollen from any flower it sees rather than going on a long journey to search for a special type of flower. However, the survival of plants depends on the bees looking for only one type of flower at a time. The design of bees, then, is more helpful to plants than it is to the bees themselves! This gives us strong evidence that bees did not come about by evolution. They were created by God, and they were created for the special purpose of helping flowers to survive. God's majesty and power are illustrated by even the tiny bee!

Tell someone everything you remember about pollination. Remember to include the special way that God designed bees to help pollinate flowers. Also remember to tell the person how pollination gives us evidence that the days in Genesis were 24 hours long.

A Bee's Landing Pad

Did you know that when helicopters land, they must have a large flat surface on which to land? When people design and build such a place for a helicopter, it is called a **landing pad**. Well, many flowers are specially designed by God to attract bees. Because bees need a place to stand when they stop to get nectar, each flower made to attract bees has a good landing pad. Of course, a good landing pad is not enough. The flower must make its nectar available to the bee, so the flower must also be large enough for the bee's head to fit inside.

This flower has an excellent landing pad for a bee.

Once a bee lands on a flower, he usually walks toward the center to get the pollen. Once at the center, he sticks his head deep inside to gather the nectar and uses his special legs to collect and store the pollen. You can be sure that if the flower has a large landing pad, it is likely designed to attract bees. Some flowers are amazing in their creation, showing us the wonderful imagination of our Creator! The orchid is one such flower.

Look at the pictures below. On the left, you see a picture of a lady slipper orchid. It has a deep pocket that is actually a bee trap. When a bee crawls down into the flower to get the nectar, the pocket on the flower closes shut. As a result, the bee is stuck for a while, wiggling and squirming, getting pollen all over itself. The bee eventually finds a small opening near the top of the orchid, and it gets out so that it can get trapped inside another lady slipper, where it will transfer that pollen to the new lady slipper's stigma.

A bee orchid (the one on the right) is another delightfully-designed flower, because it looks and smells just like a female bumblebee! This attracts male

Lady Slipper Orchid

Bee Orchid

bumblebees, which come to the flower for a friendly meeting. Before the male bumble bee realizes he has been tricked, the orchid gets pollinated! A few other orchids look and smell like insects in order to attract pollinators, and others have traps that keep the bee from escaping until it pollinates the flower.

This orchid attracts flies and gnats with a horrible smell.

One kind of orchid stinks like the rotten food a fly or gnat would want, attracting hordes of flies and gnats to its smelly nectaries. These flies and gnats search around for the food that they want, pollinating the flower in the process. The insects then leave in disgust, because they cannot find the meal that they want. You see, they don't want nectar. They want rotten food, and there is no rotten food in these orchids.   If you smell a flower that simply stinks, you know it was designed for the flies and gnats of the world to pollinate.

Creation Confirmation

Orchids give us further evidence against evolution. Flowers don't use nectar for themselves. They only use it to attract animals to help them in pollination. Flowers spend a lot of energy making nectar that just gets eaten by the animals. Since orchids like the bee orchid get pollinated without actually feeding the animals, survival is easier for them. They don't have to keep making food for animals. Evolution would say that since these orchids have an easier time surviving than orchids that actually feed animals, they should be the main kind of orchids in creation. Why, then, are they rare compared to the other orchids? Only a few orchids attract animals by imitation. Most of them use a lot of energy making food for animals in order to attract them. The fact that most orchids (and flowers in general) produce nectar for animals to eat shows that God intended flowers and animals to work together to survive.

Orchid Notebook Activity

Study the orchids on the next page. They are amazing flowers. God's design for each is specific and spectacular. Some look like dragons, others like different creatures. Now it's your turn! Using crayons or colored pencils, design a flower that looks like a living creature. Think of the special ways it will get pollinated and write that on a separate piece of a paper. Put your work in your notebook.

Flower Color

Think about what you have learned so far. All of the bees in a hive look for one kind of flower at a time. In addition, bees need a landing pad to stand on while they are gathering nectar and pollen. Finally, bees are attracted to flowers that smell nice. God gave bees the ability to smell, and just like you and me, bees like things that smell sweet.

Bees are attracted to flowers by their smell, their color, and the presence of a landing pad.

There is one more thing that attracts bees to flowers: color! Bees love flowers that are white, yellow, orange, blue, pink, and all colors in between. If the flower is all red, however, bees don't bother much with it unless it smells really nice. Why is that? Because bees can't see the color red! I will try to explain why.

Did you know that the rainbow contains all of the colors that we can see? The set of colors in the rainbow (red, orange, yellow, green, blue, indigo, and violet) is called the **visible spectrum** (spek' trum). "Visible" means that it can be seen. Those colors, then, are the colors of light that we can see. Did you know that there is a lot of light that we cannot see? That's right. You and I can only see *some* of the light that comes from the sun.

There are many kinds of light that come from the sun that we just cannot see. Two of these kinds of light are **infrared** (in' fruh red) **light** and **ultraviolet** (uhl' truh vie' uh let) **light**. The sun produces these kinds of light as well, but we cannot see them. Even though we can't see them, they are certainly there!

Look at the drawing on the right. Do you see the rays coming from the sun? Notice that some of those rays form the visible spectrum that is in the middle of the drawing. Remember, that's the light we can see. However, notice that on both sides of the visible spectrum, there is infrared light and ultraviolet light. This non-visible light is not seen by human eyes, but it is there. In the drawing, the infrared and ultraviolet light are given colors, but they are not really colored. Since we cannot see them, they do not have color. If we can't see them, how do we know they are there? Special equipment allows us to detect the presence of this non-visible light.

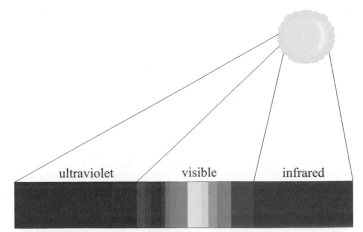

The sun shines with many different kinds of light, including light that we can see and light that we cannot see.

Bees have a different visible spectrum than we do. They cannot see any of the colors at the red end of our visible spectrum. However, bees can see colors very well at the violet end of our visible spectrum. They can also see some of the light that is not visible to you and me. They can actually see ultraviolet light! Isn't it amazing that God created creatures that can see light that we cannot see? If you wonder why He did that, read on!

Nectar Guides

Flowers have special patterns on their petals which tell the bees and butterflies exactly where their nectar is stored. These special designs "point" the insect toward the center of the flower. We call these patterns **nectar guides**. Have you ever seen a dart board with a bulls-eye in the middle? That is what a flower's nectar guide seems like for the insect. The bulls-eye is the center of the flower, where the nectar is hidden.

Certain flowers have very obvious nectar guides. The pansies pictured below have a clear pattern that points the bee directly to where it can find the nectar. Speaking of pointing out where the nectar is, look at the orchid pictured below. It actually seems to have a little "arrow" pointing to the center of the flower. The "arrow" tells the bee to go in that direction to find nectar.

These pansies show bees where they can find nectar.   This orchid "points" to where the nectar is.

Although we can see the nectar guides on these flowers, God has designed some nectar guides that only bees and certain other insects can see. This is because many nectar guides are visible only to creatures that can see ultraviolet light.

A Bee's Ultraviolet Vision

Now you know why God created bees with the ability to see ultraviolet light! When a bee sees the nectar guides with its ultraviolet vision, it knows where to go to get the nectar.

I want you to get an idea of what these ultraviolet nectar guides look like. Look at the two pictures below. They are black-and-white photos of the same flowers. The photo on the left, however, was taken with visible light. It is a black-and-white version of the flowers as we see them. The photo on the right was taken with ultraviolet light. As a result, this is how a bee sees those same flowers. Notice what the bee sees. It sees nectar patterns that we cannot see. This allows the bee to find the nectar easily, even though you and I might have a harder time finding it. That's okay, though. You and I don't need the nectar to survive.

Black-and-white version of the way we see these flowers.

Black-and-white version of the way a bee sees these flowers.

Just because this is so neat, I want you to look at two more pictures. The picture on the left is the way we see the flower. Now, of course, we would really see the flower in color, but the camera that took the photograph was using black-and-white film. The picture on the right is the way a bee would see the flower. Once again, the bee can see the nectar guides that we cannot see.

Black-and-white version of the way we see this flower.

Black-and-white version of the way a bee sees this flower.

Getting the Pollen

The nectar in a flower is usually stored near the center. As a bee seeks out the nectar, it gets pollen on its body. This happens because as a bee moves toward the nectar, the pollen on the anther (the tip of the stamen) rubs onto the bee. This ensures that the pollen will touch the bee and stick to its furry little body.

Sometimes the stamen is on a little trigger that flings the anther toward the place where the petal was touched. This throws pollen onto the bee. Other flowers are designed so that the bee must walk by the stigma, rubbing its body against it before it can walk down to the nectaries, where the nectar is stored.

The yellow "dust" that you see on this bee's legs is pollen that got on the bee when it was getting nectar from a flower.

Next time you are out in nature or at a plant nursery, study each flower carefully and try to guess how the pollen will get on a bee that visits the flower looking for nectar. Now remember, that's only part of the pollination process. In order for pollination to happen, the pollen from one flower must get onto the stigma (the top of the carpel) of another flower. As you study flowers, try to guess how the pollen that is already on the bee will get to the stigma. If you see some interesting flowers, illustrate them for your notebook and keep a record of your thoughts about the flower.

To get to the nectar in this flower, an insect will have to go through the stamens.

To help you lock all this new information into your memory, use your own words to explain the things you have learned about orchids, visible and non-visible light, and nectar guides.

Project
Flower Pollination

You will need:

♦ Two flowers that are still on their plants. (They should be on two separate plants of the same type. If you have a squash plant, you only need one flower.)

♦ A cotton swab (like a Q-tip®)

1. Rub the cotton swab in the anthers of the flower. Do you remember what the anthers are? They are on top of the stamens, which are the male parts of the flower.

2. Pull the cotton swab out of the flower. Is it covered with pollen? Pollen usually looks like yellow dust. If it is not covered with pollen, rub it in the anthers some more.

3. Once you get pollen on your cotton swab, rub the stigma of the *other* flower with the cotton swab. Your goal is to get some of the pollen from the cotton swab onto the stigma. If you are using a single squash flower, do the same thing, but just use the one flower. Do you see how easy it is to pollinate flowers?

4. Watch carefully over the next few weeks to see if a fruit begins to grow from the flower you pollinated. If you really did succeed in getting pollen from one flower to the stigma of another flower (or the same flower in the case of squash), a fruit should form, because fruits contain seeds, and pollination is supposed to produce seeds. The fruit will be any container that has seeds inside. It might be just a big green swelling, or it could be a little berry. **DO NOT TRY TO EAT THE FRUIT!** Many fruits cannot be eaten by people.

5. Write down what you did for your notebook. Illustrate a picture of yourself pollinating the flowers with a Q-tip. Leave room to record the results of your pollination experiment!

If your pollination experiment goes well, you will start with a flower like this…

…and end up with a fruit like this!

Butterflies

Butterflies spark joy and excitement in everyone they encounter. God must have had a wonderful time planning the colors and patterns on the butterflies of the world. Butterflies are so delightful that many people plant gardens specifically to attract butterflies. They grow the plants caterpillars will eat so that butterflies will lay their eggs on them. They also plant the flowering plants that are most loved by butterflies. They do this in the hope of attracting butterflies so that they can enjoy watching these beautiful insects.

Do you know what butterflies live in your area? If you live in the U.S. or Canada, the painted lady is a common butterfly in your area. Would you like to build a butterfly garden so that butterflies will spend time in your yard? You can even build a butterfly garden in containers, or pots. At the end of this lesson is a list of butterflies, their favorite flowers, and what their caterpillars must have to eat. You can begin an outdoor butterfly garden this spring or summer.

Butterflies need flowers to survive. They must have the sweet nectar for food. Although butterflies pollinate many of the same flowers that bees pollinate, certain flowers are especially meant for butterflies.

Like bees, butterflies must have a landing pad, but because butterfly legs are thin, they do not need a large landing pad. Also, the flower doesn't need to be large enough for the head of the butterfly, because the butterfly collects nectar with a long, curly "straw" called a **proboscis** (pro bah' skus). The butterfly lands upon the flower and uncurls its long proboscis, which delves deep into the flower and sucks up the nectar.

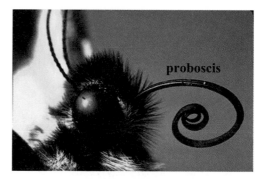

proboscis

When you see a flower that is teeny tiny, with a long, thin neck below the opening, you can be certain that it is especially meant for butterflies to pollinate. One such flower is called the butterfly bush, or buddleia (bud lee' uh). If you put flowering plants like the butterfly bush in your garden, you will probably have butterfly guests all summer long. Look for butterflies during warm days, for they must have the warm sun upon their bodies to be able to fly. When they get too cool, they can no longer move. They rest all night until the sun warms them up again the next day. In the winter, they either move to warmer climates or hibernate like a bear! Butterflies are important pollinators. Without them, many flowers wouldn't be able to make seeds.

Moths

Have you ever noticed that there are certain flowers that have no scent during the day but have a sweet smell at night? In the heat of the day, you can't smell these flowers even if you stick your nose

inside of them. As the day cools and evening approaches, however, they begin to emit a sweet, strong smell. If you take an early morning walk before the day warms up, you can still smell them as you pass by.

Usually, these special night-aroma plants are very light in color, making them easier to see at night. Light colors are easier to see at night than dark colors. That is why you should wear white clothes on evening walks, so that car and truck drivers can more easily see you.

Notice how the moth continues to fly while it sucks nectar from these flowers.

Why would God make flowers like that? Well, He designed them to attract pollinators at night. What pollinators do these flowers attract? They attract moths!

Most moths are **nocturnal** (nahk turn' uhl). That means they sleep during the day and come out at night. A moth uses it proboscis to collect nectar just as a butterfly does. One big difference between moths and butterflies, however, is that moths do not always land on the flower to get to the nectar. They often hover near the flower and flap their wings vigorously in midair while they sip the nectar. Because of this, moth-pollinated flowers don't need a landing pad. In fact, some moth-pollinated flowers are pointing downward, making it easier for the flying moth to collect nectar.

Notice the yucca flowers in the picture on the right; they are upside down! Moth-pollinated flowers often have the stamen near the tip of the flower to make certain a hovering moth gets pollen on it. They also have carpels close to the tip. Can you guess why?

Look for moth-pollinated flowers when you go on evening or early morning nature hikes. Make illustrations of them and write down why you believe they are designed to be pollinated by moths.

These yucca flowers are ideal for moth pollination because they hang upside down.

Hummingbirds

Not only do insects help flowers to pollinate, some birds do as well. The hummingbird is a very beautiful sight to see. The sweet little hummingbird is probably more exciting to see than a

butterfly! The hummingbird, like the butterfly, loves nectar. God did not give most birds a good sense of smell, so a wonderful-smelling flower isn't what the hummingbird is looking for. They are attracted to color. Guess what color the hummingbird loves the most? Red!

Have you ever seen a hummingbird feeder? What color was it? If you have seen one, it was red! Although a bee cannot see red, birds can see red very well. So, when you see a big red flower, God might have made it to feed hummingbirds, and if it smells nice, butterflies and bees might be invited guests as well.

As this hummingbird feeds from the flower, its wings beat so quickly that they are a blur.

Like the moth, the hummingbird hovers over the flower as it drinks. As it hovers in place, its wings flap so quickly that you and I see them as one big blur! A hummingbird might shove its entire head down into the flower to sip the nectar. When it pulls its head out, guess what color its head can be? All covered with pollen, its head turns yellow, like a canary's head! It is just another one of the delightful ways that God has designed flowers to get pollinated, while giving life-sustaining nectar to the animals. Many times, pollen is rubbed onto the hummingbird's little pointy beak. That is another way it transfers pollen from one flower to another.

If you place a hummingbird feeder outside your window, you are likely to see many of these amazing creatures on their search for a sweet drink. It might be fun to plant some favorite hummingbird flowers nearby as well, such as cypress vine (red), native trumpet vine, morning glories (red), coral honeysuckle (red), and holleyhock.

This hummingbird is attracted to the red base in the hummingbird feeder.

Believe it or not, the very best way to get the hummingbirds to choose your yard for a visit is to place bright red artificial flowers in places that a passing hummingbird might see. The birds have keen sight for bright red objects and will come to investigate. If you have a trail of artificial red flowers leading them toward your hummingbird feeder, they will follow your trail and end up where you want them. Seeing the bright red from afar, they will come in to inspect. They will then be led, flower-by-flower, in a treasure hunt for your feeder!

Bat Pollinators

Like most moths, bats are nocturnal. That means they come out at night after resting all day. Some bat species pollinate flowers. The flowers they visit are aromatic at night. That means they are really smelly when the sun goes down, similar to the moth-pollinated flowers. However, bats are not looking for a sweet smell; they prefer musty or sour odors.

This bat is pollinating this flower.

Bat-pollinated flowers tend to be pale, and they typically have a strong odor at night. Plants that are pollinated by bats must be strong and sturdy to support the little mammal as it climbs on the branch of the flower bush. They also have very few leaves, so they don't get in the way of the bat as he seeks the flower. A cactus plant is a great flowering plant for a bat. It has sturdy limbs, no leaves, and big flowers. Of course, the bat has to keep clear of a cactus's prickles, lest it get them stuck in its skin.

Explain in your own words what you remember about how butterflies, moths, hummingbirds, and bats pollinate flowers.

Notebook Activity

Make a notebook page for each type of pollinator we discussed (bees, moths, hummingbirds, and bats). On each page, draw the pollinator and write down (or dictate to your parent / teacher) the interesting things you learned about it.

Wind Pollination

Have you ever noticed that during a certain time of year, you can find a fine, yellow dust on everything outside? What do you think that dust is? It's pollen, of course! The reason that it is all over the place is because God designed some plants to get pollinated by the wind.

How can plants get pollinated by the wind? Well, consider trees. Some trees develop little catkin flowers. Do you see the catkins in the picture on the right? Do they look familiar to you? Most people don't realize that a catkin is a flower. It's a male flower, because it has only stamens. It does not have carpels. The abundance of catkin flowers a tree

Catkins are the male flowers of a tree.

produces is often amazing. Because they blend in quite well with the tree, we often don't realize how many there are. Have you noticed the hundreds of little catkins that lie upon the ground in early summer?

After the catkins form and pollen covers their tiny stamens, the pollen blows off the catkins with every passing breeze. The pollen goes gliding through the air, much of it eventually landing on the ground. Some of the pollen, however, may just blow onto another tree of the same kind nearby. That tree might have female flowers with little sticky carpels (but no stamens) ready to receive the pollen that blows by.

The catkin produces much more pollen than a regular flower does, because it needs to cover the air with pollen in the hopes of it landing on a nearby tree. After all, since bees tend to look for only one type of flower at a time, a bee-pollinated flower does not need to produce a lot of pollen. The bee efficiently carries the pollen to another flower of the same type. Since wind pollination is not as efficient, wind-pollinated plants must produce a lot more pollen. The Lord designed the catkin stamens to produce an overabundance of pollen to ensure that there will be another generation of trees born from the seeds.

Flowers that are wind pollinated don't have to be pretty, and they usually are not. Grass flowers and the flowers of many trees are usually not lovely to behold. Often they are rather greenish or brown in color, the same as the rest of the plant. Most people do not even realize that the little tips on the grass in their yard are flowers. They can sometimes look like little green wheat grains or little helicopter blades sitting on your grass.

The things that appear to be wheat grains on this grass are actually flowers.

Why Most Flowers Do Not Self-Pollinate

As I told you before, most flowers cannot self-pollinate. The pollen from one plant must be transferred to the carpel of another plant in order for pollination to actually occur. How did God design flowers to keep from self-pollinating since the stamen and the carpel are right next to one another? Not surprisingly, He did it in several different ways. In some plants, God designed the male and female flower parts to develop, or mature, at different times. That way, the carpel on a plant will not be ready to accept pollen when the stamens on the same plant release their pollen. On another plant of the same type, the carpels will be ready to accept pollen before its stamens are ready to release pollen. That way, when the first plant releases pollen, it can only be accepted by the carpels on the other plant. Lilies are an example of a plant whose carpels and stamens mature at different times.

God keeps other plants from self-pollination by giving the plant an "allergy" to its own pollen. The plant's carpel will happily accept pollen from another plant of the same type, but it cannot accept its own pollen, because it is essentially "allergic" to its own pollen! The tobacco plant is like this. It can actually recognize its own pollen because of special chemicals in the pollen, and it rejects its own pollen. However, a different tobacco plant produces pollen with slightly different chemicals, so a tobacco plant is not allergic to the pollen from *other* tobacco plants.

In some plants, like holly plants, there are stamens on one plant and carpels on another plant. Because of this, a holly plant that produces pollen cannot accept pollen, because it has no carpels. In the same way, a holly plant that has carpels will never produce pollen, because it has no stamens. That way, it is impossible for a holly plant to pollinate itself. If a plant produces flowers with just stamens or just carpels, the flowers are called **imperfect flowers**. Imperfect flowers are not any less ideal than other flowers, we just use that term. A holly plant's imperfect flowers are ideal for the holly plant.

It is important to understand what it means if a plant cannot self-pollinate. Consider roses. Many species of rose will not self-pollinate. That means that if I have the only rose bush in the entire city, it will never make any more seeds for any more rose bushes. If I want more rose bushes, I'd better plant more than one rose bush to begin with. That way, one rose bush can pollinate the other one, and the roses will then develop into fruits, called "rose hips," which will contain seeds for more rose bushes.

Self-Pollination

Even though most plants cannot self-pollinate, God did design a few varieties of plants to be self-pollinators. That means a single plant can pollinate itself! Of course, a plant that self-pollinates can also be pollinated by another plant, so a plant that *can* self-pollinate does not *have to* self-pollinate. However, self-pollination is obviously the easiest way to get pollinated. The Lord created only some plants to self-pollinate, and wouldn't you know it, many of those plants are the foods we eat!

Yes, indeed! The Lord designed self-pollination to help out mankind. Self-pollination is the method of pollination for many food crops. Wheat, barley, rice, and oats can all self-pollinate. Beans, peas, soybeans, peanuts, eggplant, lettuce, peppers, and tomatoes can as well. These are all foods that people around the world depend on to live!

Tomato plants can self-pollinate, making it easy for them to reproduce. That makes it easy for us to grow lots of tomatoes!

That means that if I only had one wheat seed, I could still grow an entire crop of wheat after a few years. It is the same with the other self-pollinators! God sure takes care of people doesn't He? The Bible tells us that man is the most important of all of God's creation, for we are the only creation made in the image of God. God loves us all deeply and desires for us to survive the sometimes difficult times here on earth. Because of this, He has provided for us in many ways, including making our food easier to grow!

The Pollinated Flower

Once a flower has been pollinated, the petals, now finished with their work of attracting guests to their home, dry up and fall off. The flower can then spend all its energy not on looking and smelling just right, but on manufacturing the seeds within. Another important reason God made the flower petals die after pollination is so that all the other flowers on the bush get an equal chance to be pollinated. If flowers still looked lovely after they were pollinated, birds, bees, and butterflies may spend their visit on flowers that don't need pollination. Fewer seeds would be made if this happened. God really thought of everything, didn't He!

As the petals fall off, the carpel's ovary begins to ripen, making seeds and encasing those seeds in a fruit. The fruit protects the seeds, but it also helps the seeds get away from the parent tree. After all, if the seeds from a tree just fall on the ground next to the tree, it will be hard for them to grow. Their parent tree is using the sunlight, soil, and water in that area. It would be easier for the new tree to grow if it were far from its parent. How does the fruit accomplish this? You will learn all about that in the next lesson.

If these cherry blossoms are successfully pollinated, they will develop into delicious cherries, each of which contains a seed that can grow into a new cherry tree.

What Do You Remember?

What was the most interesting thing you learned today? What would you like to remember of all that you learned? Explain wind pollination and self-pollination to someone else. Can you also explain why a flower petal dries up and falls off after it has been pollinated?

Notebook Activities

Make illustrations of some of the most interesting things you learned today for your notebook. Title your pages and, if you can, write down what you want to remember about each thing you learned.

Comic Strip Activity

Younger Students: Make up a story about a flower. Your story should start with the flower opening up, waiting to be pollinated. In your story, tell how the flower is pollinated (by bees, butterflies, wind, etc.), and then tell about it becoming a fruit. Describe the fruit that the flower becomes, and finally, tell how the fruit gets carried away from its parent plant.

Older Students: Have you ever seen a comic strip? It is a story told inside little boxes. If you have a newspaper in your house, you can see what a comic strip looks like. Today you are going to make a comic strip called "The Life of a Flower." This comic strip should tell about the life of a flower, from the time it opens up until the time its fruit has developed.

Make a sketch on a piece of paper of what you will put in each box before you do the real thing. When you are ready to do the real thing, make boxes like those in a comic strip. Your comic strip can have as many boxes as you wish, as long as there are at least four. Here are what comic strip boxes look like:

Each box should contain an illustration and some words explaining the illustration. For example, your first box might contain a drawing of a beautiful flower, with an explanation saying something like, "The flower opened up, using its beauty and wonderful scent to attract a pollinator."

Project
Make a Butterfly Garden

In order to make a butterfly garden, you will need to grow the plants that meet the needs of the butterfly in each stage of its life: the egg, caterpillar, chrysalis (cocoon), and adult butterfly. Butterflies will lay their eggs only on plants that its caterpillar will eat. Each species of caterpillar eats different plants. While in the chrysalis, the butterfly does not eat; however, it needs a sheltered environment. It usually hangs from a twig and is hidden from view by its coloring.

Each kind of butterfly caterpillar must have a particular kind of food. So, you must learn which butterflies are common to your area. If you have trouble learning the species common to your area, and you live in the United States or Canada, you can build a garden for these very common species: painted ladies, swallowtails, whites and sulphurs, gossamer-wing butterflies, brush-footed butterflies, and skippers. Butterflies must have sunlight to warm their bodies. If it gets too cool, they are unable to move. Because of this, it is best to plant these flowers in a sunny place.

Once you learn which types of butterflies are common to your region, you need to grow two types of plants. First, you need to grow the kinds of plants that produce nectar which butterflies enjoy eating. Second, you will need to grow the kinds of plants on which the butterflies will lay eggs. These would be plants that the caterpillars enjoy eating. Since each species of butterfly tends to lay its eggs on specific plants, you need to make sure that you get the right kinds of plants. Your local nursery will be happy to help you, as many people ask them the same questions you will need answered. I have included some information below to help you.

Plants that make flowers which produce nectar that most butterflies enjoy eating: butterfly bush, lantana, zinnia, bee balm, purple coneflower, penta, sage, milkweed or butterfly weed, lilac, sunflower, marjoram

Plants and Trees with Leaves That are Eaten by the Caterpillars of Different Species of Butterflies

Butterfly	Plant	Butterfly	Plant	Butterfly	Plant
painted lady	thistle	greater and lesser fritillaries	violet	California sister	live oak
tiger swallowtail	tulip tree	orange-barred sulphur	pea plants, alfalfa	American copper	sheep sorrel
spicebush swallowtail	sassafras, spicebush	cloudless sulphur	wild senna	eastern tailed blue, orange-bordered blue	legumes
anise swallowtail	parsnips, fennel, carrots, parsley	question mark and zephyr	elm	common blue	dogwood flower
pipevine swallowtail	pipevine	fawn	birch	marine blue	wisteria, alfalfa, legumes
black swallowtail	fennel, dill, carrots, parsley, parsnips	southern dogface	wild indigo, clover	southern cloudy wing, northern cloudy wing	clover
common buckeye	snapdragon	great southern white	mustard	sara orange tip	wild mustard
monarch	milkweed, butterfly weed	julia, gulf fritillary, zebras	passion flower leaf	silver spotted skipper	wisteria
filed crescent	aster	mourning cloak	elm, willow, poplar	grizzled skipper, west coast lady	mallows

Your Butterfly Garden

You can grow the seeds in your light hut and then transplant them outside into healthy soil when they are big and sturdy. Healthy soil is filled with organic materials. It is usually dark brown to black in color. When you squeeze it into a ball in your hands, it holds it shape until you toss it down on the ground, at which point it breaks apart. Bad soil is light brown and can't hold its shape when you squeeze it. Clay that holds its shape even when tossed on the ground is also bad soil.

If you are planting in a container garden, you can use separate pots or a plastic baby pool for all the plants. Put a layer of pebbles on the bottom of the container or containers and good soil on top of the pebbles. Make sure to choose a spot that gets plenty of sun. Transplant your plants carefully and water them daily until they are established in the soil. Don't over water, because the roots need air to breathe and can drown with too much water. Once the plant is established, water only when the soil is no longer moist to the touch.

You can fertilize your garden with compost. This is a great time to do some research on how to begin a compost pile and what to put in it. Compost is a very-nutrient rich fertilizer that will keep your plants healthy.

Lesson 5
Fruits

We learned a lot about flowers in the previous two lessons. We learned how a flower makes seeds as a result of pollination, and we learned all about God's special pollinators. But wait! If you can believe it, there's more to this amazing process! After the flower gets pollinated, it has one more job to do. It has to grow its seeds inside a fruit!

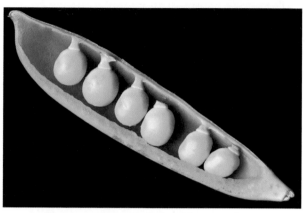
The pea pod is the fruit of the pea plant.

After pollination, the flower's ovary begins to swell and swell as the seeds within it mature. To protect the seeds, the ovary forms a fruit around them. Sometimes the ovaries grow into flat pods, such as a pea pod. Sometimes they get large and plump, forming a fruit like a tomato. They can grow a furry tuft, or a parachute that will help the seeds float in the wind. Other times, the ovaries form into little hard shells, such as walnuts. Regardless of how a plant's ovary develops into a fruit, the fruit is the container for the plant's seed. Remember that "angiosperm" means "seed container." We are now going to look closely at these seed containers.

All these containers are called "fruits," even though we don't often think of pea pods and nuts as fruits. When someone says "fruit," we usually think of things like apples and oranges. However, everything that grows from a pollinated flower and contains seeds is considered a fruit. This means that an acorn is really a fruit. It means that a sunflower seed is a fruit as well! Many things that we would never think of as fruits are, indeed, fruits. This is a very important point. Sometimes we use words in our everyday language that are not scientifically correct. For example, most people think of tomatoes as vegetables, but they are not vegetables. What do you see when you cut into a tomato? You see seeds. That means the tomato is a container for seeds, which

Tomatoes contain seeds, so they are fruits.

makes it a fruit. Try to remember that everything that serves as a container for the seed is a fruit. Have you ever watched a program called "Veggie Tales?" Although the show is supposed to be about vegetables, many of the characters (like Larry the cucumber and Bob the tomato) are fruits!

If many of the things we think of as vegetables are actually fruits, I bet you are wondering what exactly a vegetable is. A vegetable is any edible part of a plant that does not have seeds. For example, lettuce leaves are vegetables, since they do not contain seeds. The buds and stems of a broccoli plant are vegetables, because they do not contain seeds. Many of the vegetables we eat are actually from the roots of plants as well. Carrots and potatoes, for example, are parts of the root systems of their plants. Once again, since they have no seeds, they are also vegetables.

Broccoli is a vegetable because it does not contain seeds.

Now that you know the proper way to distinguish between fruits and vegetables, let's go back to talking about fruits. Remember, a fruit is a container for seeds. It is a vessel in which seeds are placed and then eventually spread to other places. There are many, many different kinds of these seed containers, and each comes with its own special way of spreading its seeds to other places.

Why would God create so many different kinds of fruits? The design of fruits in creation is a beautiful picture of God's wisdom at work. Not only does the variety of fruits give man and animals

Fruits are used by animals as a nutritious food source.

many healthy foods to eat, God knew that there is only so much nutrition in one plot of soil. Do you realize that the plant uses the nutrients from the soil, and if they are not replenished, the soil can lose all its nutrients because the plants can use them up?

Although God has designed special processes by which dead animals and plants decompose and refill the soil with nutrients for plants, the supply of nutrients in each plot of ground is still limited. Sometimes, one spot of land can only support one healthy plant. The mother plant that produces seeds shouldn't have to struggle with her own offspring for the nutrients in the soil. If they were to battle with one another over water and nutrients, the mother plant with her well-developed roots would likely win. As a result, the baby plant would not be able to get enough nutrition and would die or be very unhealthy. On the other hand, if the mother plant was old and weak, the baby plant could grow vigorously and suck up all the nutrients, starving its mother of what she needs, eventually killing her.

The Lord God made special plans in His creation so that this would not happen. He chose to make few seeds that would drop straight down from the parent plant onto the same plot of soil. Instead, God built little seed houses called fruits. He gave each fruit a special and unique job of moving the seed to a new plot of ground. Sometimes the fruit is designed to move the seeds just a small distance away, and sometimes the fruit is designed to move the seeds very, very far away.

The process of getting the seeds from the parent plant to a new location is called **seed dispersal**. "Dispersal" means "spreading" or "scattering." Have you ever dispersed anything? What have you dispersed? The mail carrier disperses mail; rain clouds disperse rain; fruits disperse seeds.

There are five different ways that seeds are dispersed: humans, water, wind, animals, and mechanical means. Can you guess how each of these works? Think about each one for a moment and make your best hypothesis (guess). We will then see if you are correct as we read on.

Fruits that are dispersed by water can float. The plants that produce them usually grow near rivers, oceans, and streams. Human dispersal is caused when people harvest seeds and then plant them to grow crops for food and gardens for beauty. Fruits that are wind-dispersed float easily in the breeze. Fruits that are animal-dispersed are carried off by animals. Finally, mechanical dispersal is a wonderful mechanism that God designed. In this mechanism, the fruit is like a little machine that flings the seeds out when they are ready.

So you see that fruits are God's special moving vans. They come in all shapes and sizes. They all have a different way that they move their cargo, the seeds. One thing is the same with them all: they are all designed to be the movers of the seeds. Let's explore each of the methods of seed dispersal. After that, we will study the different names for the fruits that God created.

Fruits are like moving vans that relocate seeds to new areas.

Human Dispersal

Human dispersal is often ignored by scientists when discussing the different methods of seed dispersal. Nevertheless, when God created the earth, He planned for many kinds of seeds to be mainly dispersed by humans. These seeds would be used to grow food for people. Farmers raise many plants for food, and they even raise some plants to give us what we need to make clothing.

Some textbooks say that humans slowly learned how to do this, but that is just not true. The Bible tells us that God put Adam in the Garden of Eden to care for it (Gen 2:15), so He must have taught Adam how to grow and care for plants. Adam passed this skill on to his children, who passed it on their children, and so on. Before Adam sinned, farming was easier. After he sinned, one of the curses was that farming became very difficult and man must work very hard to grow food (Gen 3:17-19).

As we can see, farming was always a part of God's great plan for humankind. Of course, all of the seeds that are primarily dispersed by humans have other methods of dispersal as well. Even though this is the case, we should remember that God designed farming as a way for us to get much of the food that we need to survive. As a result, humans are definitely a big part of the way some seeds are dispersed.

Farming has always been a part of God's plan for people.

Water Dispersal

Have you ever seen living plants growing in water? The water lily is an example of such a plant. Water lilies have beautiful flowers. When the flowers are pollinated, they create a fruit that floats in the water for a while and then drops down to the bottom to take root on the floor of the pond. The seeds of water lilies have been specially created to be dispersed and germinate in water.

Water lilies use water to disperse their seeds.

There are many other plants that produce seeds that can float, and they use this as their primary method of seed dispersal. Once the seed falls into the water, it will be carried a long distance before it finds a resting place to grow.

The palm tree is a great example of a plant that God designed to disperse its seeds by water. Have you ever noticed that palm trees often grow near oceans? Ocean currents are powerful and stretch from one continent to another. This is the road the palm tree uses to move its seeds (which we call coconuts) to their new home. When a coconut lands in the ocean, it can float a long time, being carried thousands of miles away,

Palm trees use water to disperse their coconuts.

even to a new continent, to grow.   If you ever buy a coconut from the store, fill up your sink with water, put in the coconut, and watch how it floats.

If you have ever been to Florida and seen a mangrove tree, you will notice they live right there in the water. Their seeds fall from the tree and will grow roots as soon as they touch any kind of soil. During low tide, they may fall in soil rather than water and start growing right where they fell. If the water level is high, however, they can be carried far away from where they fell. Mangrove trees are often the beginning of what will one day be a small island. As dirt and debris collect in their roots, little bodies of land are formed.

Mangrove trees grow right out of the water.

Most nuts, such as the acorn, walnut, and pecan are designed to be dispersed by both water and animals. The main way that they are dispersed by water is during flood times, or if their plants grow near a river or stream. Many nut trees can be found in areas that have a lot of flooding or in areas where they hang over streams or rivers. Although seed dispersal is important to trees, it is not as important for them as it is for other plants. You see, many trees have roots that are able to grow a long way from the tree to find a nutritious soil and plenty of water.

What Do You Remember?

What is the main purpose of fruits? What is the difference between a fruit and a vegetable? Describe what seed dispersal means. Explain the two methods of dispersal that we have discussed so far.

Wind Dispersal

The tufts on the seeds of this dandelion allow them to be carried away by the wind.

God has also designed some fruits to be dispersed by the wind. What do you think is an important characteristic for a wind-dispersed seed? It can't be heavy like a walnut or a coconut! It must be able to float easily in the breeze. There are several designs God made for wind dispersal. He made some seeds so that they grow a little tuft or parachute on top, like milkweed and dandelion seeds.

God also designed some seeds to be small and light, almost like dust. Orchid seeds and poppy seeds are like that. They are so light that they float easily in the breeze. Poppy seeds are contained in a little capsule that has little windows around the top. On a windy day, the poppy fruit capsule will sway from side to side, shaking out the tiny little seeds from the windows of the capsule, like a salt shaker. The seeds are so light that they can float for a short distance before they settle to the ground. Isn't that amazing?

Another kind of fruit that God designed to be wind-dispersed is the maple tree fruit. The maple tree develops little **schizocarps** (skit' suh karps), which are two-sided winged fruits. They are usually called **samaras** (suh' mah rus). They are light little fruits that fly off the tree with a strong wind. Their little wing structures help them to stay in the air until they have reached a new plot of ground. The elm and birch tree are also equipped with samaras that have a wing-like structure surrounding the seed. When they fall from the trees, they look like little butterflies flittering to the ground.

The maple tree's samaras have wings to help carry them in the wind.

We will be using wind-dispersed fruits in an experiment at the end of this lesson, so begin looking for a dandelion tuft and a samara like the one pictured above. Samaras can be found any time of the year on the ground near maple trees. If you are unable to get a dandelion tuft, you can purchase one through a science supply store.

Mechanical Dispersal

Have you ever seen a slingshot? It's a device that can fling a rock far away. In 1 Samuel 17:33-51, we read that David used a sling to defeat Goliath. A sling is kind of like the slingshot drawn on the right. Although the design is different, the job is the same. Both a sling and a slingshot can fling a rock much farther and faster than a person can throw a rock. God gave some fruits a natural ability to act like a slingshot and fling their seeds away when they are ripe. This is called "mechanical dispersal," because the fruit is launched from a little mechanism or "machine."

Pea pods often use mechanical dispersal. When the seeds are ready, the pod dries up. When the pod dries, the inside of the pod dries faster than the outside. This causes the pod to twist inwardly, suddenly splitting open with a violent force, rolling into a little spiral. When this spiral roll happens, it causes the seeds to fly out of the pod in all directions.

Sometimes mechanical dispersal is even more exciting than this. The touch-me-not (also called the "jewel weed"), which grows wild in the U.S., uses mechanical dispersal as well. The orange flowers that look like little jewels attract hummingbirds and butterflies for pollination. Once the flowers have been pollinated, the seeds form in little dry capsules. When the seeds are ripe and ready, the dried fruit is on a God-made trigger. When an animal or human touches the plant, the capsules burst open and spray the seeds everywhere! If it's

Notice how twisted these pea pods are. The twisting of the pea pods causes the seeds to fly out of the pods.

particularly windy, the plants can hit against one another, bursting the capsules and dispersing their seeds with each gust. If the ground is wet, the seeds might germinate where they land. The seeds might also stick to the creature that set off the trigger. This will allow them to be carried off to another location.

The fruit of the violet and the gorse (a European shrub) uses mechanical dispersal that is accompanied by a loud noise. The fruit dries into a little capsule. Then, when the seeds are ready, it

Once the flowers of this gorse bush are pollinated, the seeds will mature in capsules that snap open with a loud pop.

snaps open with a "POP!" It's been said that sitting in a field of ripe gorse capsules can be like sitting in a field with gunfire going on.

Another fruit that uses mechanical dispersal is the squirting cucumber. Its small, two-inch cucumbers are filled with slimy juice that contains the seeds. As they ripen, the pressure causes the cucumber to burst off its stalk and explosively shoot slimy liquid up to 20 feet away! The seeds spew out with the liquid, and voila! Seeds are sent to a new plot of land. These would be fun plant to grow. Their scientific name is *Ecballium elaterium*.

If you grow these plants, wait until the cucumber is nice and fat. To make the cucumber squirt, gently shake the vine, but stand back right away so you don't get slimed! You should never eat squirting cucumbers. They are not good for you. They are called cucumbers because they look like cucumbers, not because you can eat them.

There are hundreds of other fruits that use mechanical dispersal. Next time you are outside, especially near the end of the summer and in the fall when fruits are usually ripe, look for capsules and seeds that might snap open at a touch. If you find one, record what it was and what it did in your botany notebook.

Animal Dispersal

There are several ways that God planned for animals to help in seed dispersal. Have you ever wondered why God created those stickers or burrs that stick to your socks and pants when you walk through grassy fields? Well, that is a special method of seed dispersal! Inside each little sticker is the

These burrs are using a person's shoe to disperse their plant's seeds.

seed that developed from the flower of the plant. The parent plant develops the little stickers or burrs from the flower. These stickers are either tossed off the plant and onto the ground, or they stay on the plant until a passing animal (or person) gets the burr in its fur or feathers (or socks). The animal (or person) then carries the sticker to a new location, where the animal (or person) attempts to get the sticker off. Animals will gnaw, scratch, or peck at a burr for hours to remove it. The creature will then toss the burr on the ground, where it can grow a new plant far, far away from the soil that nourishes the parent plant! What a clever way to get the seeds to a new home!

Velcro®

Do you know that the person who developed Velcro was actually a scientist named George de Mestral? During a hunting vacation in Switzerland, de Mestral came home one evening and tried to remove the burrs stuck to his dog's fur. He was shocked at how difficult the burrs were to remove. That night he studied the burrs under a microscope and noted that each burr was covered with hundreds of small hooks acting like grasping hands. De Mestral decided that this God-designed burr could be made to close fabric instead of buttons and zippers. By copying the hook pattern that he saw on burrs, he developed Velcro! Velcro was named after the French words for velvet (velour) and hook (crochet). Velcro is man's imitation of God's handiwork in creation. Did you know that a two-inch square of de Mestral's Velcro is strong enough to hold a 175-pound person hanging on a wall?

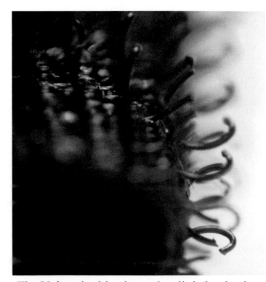

The Velcro in this picture has little hooks that imitate the hooks found on burrs.

Activity
Examining Burrs

Burrs are quite amazing. If you are able to find one, examine it carefully under a magnifying glass. You will see a special network of hooks and latches that are designed to stick onto fur. After you examine the burr, roll it onto a sock, and then try to remove it from the sock. Study it under the magnifying glass to learn why it is not easily removed. You can see now why de Mestral would want to recreate this wonderful design in his lab!

Grass

Many fruits of grasses are equipped with latches that can catch onto passing creatures as well. Spear grass has spiky tips that get lodged in passing animals or can be blown by a strong wind to a new location. The pointed fruits of spear grass have long, twisted tails (called "awns") projecting from their tips. These tails can get stuck in passing animals or can float in the wind. Once the seed hits the ground, however, the first moisture causes the awn to straighten. This causes it to move straight down into the soil. Once it dries out again, the awn twists back up. This actually screws the seed into the soil where it can germinate. The fruit of spear grass, then, not only helps disperse the seeds, it also helps plant them!

Notice the twisted tails of this spear grass fruit

Little Gardeners

This squirrel is actually a farmer!

Another way God arranged for animals to help in seed dispersal is for the animals to actually plant the seeds themselves. Yes, some animals behave like little gardeners without even knowing it. You see, animals like mice, squirrels, and jay birds gather fruits and nuts during the spring and summer, and they store them for the upcoming winter. Often, they store these fruits and nuts by burying them in the ground. Well, most of theses animals are such hard workers that they store many more fruits and nuts than they need in order to survive the winter. As a result, they leave some of their fruits and nuts buried. Those that are left buried get to become spring seedlings.

Mistletoe

Birds help with the dispersal of mistletoe in an interesting way. Mistletoe has sticky seeds inside of berries that are attractive to birds. The seeds stick to the birds' beaks when they are eating the berries. The birds fly away, only to land on another tree where they rub their beaks clean on the bark of the tree. The sticky seeds are left on the bark to grow into new mistletoe plants. You see, mistletoe does not grow in the ground. It actually grows on trees. Mistletoe is a **parasitic** (pear' uh sih' tik) plant. Parasitic plants steal nutrients from other plants. In the case of mistletoe, it steals nutrients from trees.

Seed Droppings

Have you ever wondered how so many weeds and new plants grow in your yard? We have wild strawberries growing all over our flower beds. It is because God also uses the animals to help in seed dispersal by creating lovely, tasty fruits that the animals swallow, seeds and all. They digest the soft fruit, but the seeds go through their bodies unharmed, passing out in their droppings. This is why I have wild strawberries in my yard. A bird dropped the seeds in my yard when it sat in my trees.

This hedgehog is helping to disperse apple seeds by eating an apple.

In certain parts of the earth, especially South America, bats are very important in the dispersal of seeds. Bats that live on fruit can eat up to three times their body weight in a single night. The seeds of the fruits that they eat pass through the bats in only 15 - 20 minutes. The bats then scatter them on the forest floor in their droppings. The short-tailed fruit bat in South America can scatter up to 60,000 seeds in a single night!

Fruit bats can disperse a lot of seeds!

Scattered Seeds

If you ever wondered why there are so many unwanted plants growing in your yard and garden, now you know. They were dispersed to your yard. Some were dispersed by the wind, some by mechanical means, and some by animals.

Explain in your own words wind, mechanical, and animal seed dispersal.

Fruit Types

Note to the teacher: The information in this section may be too technical for younger students. Use your own judgment as to whether or not you should cover this with your students.

Now let's explore the different types of fruit that God made. He created both fleshy and dry fruits. As you look at the list and pictures that follow, try to think of other fruits you have seen that would fit in the same category as the ones pictured.

Fleshy Fruits

Fleshy fruits are fruits that have a fleshy part between the fruit's covering and the seeds. Most of the things that you think of when you hear the word "fruits" (apples, oranges, grapes, watermelon, etc.) are fleshy fruits. Generally, when you eat one of these fruits, you are eating the "fleshy" part. The white part of an apple, for example, is the "fleshy" part of the apple. Fleshy fruits are generally put in the following categories:

Berry: If the entire fruit is fleshy, except for perhaps a thin skin, we call the fruit a berry. A berry might contain one seed or many. Grapes, avocados, and blueberries are examples of berries. They all have a thin skin, but most of the fruit is fleshy. Believe it or not, strawberries are not really berries. This is because the seed or seeds must be inside the berry. On a strawberry, the seeds are on the outside of the fruit.

Pepo (pee' po): A pepo is a modified berry. Its skin is hard and thick and is usually called a "rind." Pumpkins and watermelons are pepos.

Hesperidium (hes' per id' ee uhm): A hesperidium is another modified berry. It has a leathery skin that is not as hard as the skin of a pepo. All citrus fruit like oranges and lemons are in this category.

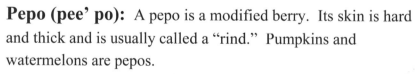

Pome (pohm): A pome is a fruit that developed a core surrounded by a fleshy tissue that can be eaten. The core is usually not eaten. This is different from a berry, in which the seeds are embedded in the fleshy part, not separated from it by a core. Apples and pears are pomes.

Drupe: A drupe is a fleshy fruit with a hard stone surrounding the seed. We often call this stone the "pit" of the fruit. Peaches and olives, for example, are drupes. It actually turns out that the almond fruit is a drupe as well. When you eat an almond, however, the fruit has actually been removed. What you eat is the seed, or the "pit" of the almond fruit.

Dry Fruits

Dry fruits are fruits that have no fleshy part between the fruit's outer layer and the seed. Dry fruits are usually put in the following categories:

Grain or caryopsis (ka ree op' sis): This is a very small, one-seeded fruit. The seed is coated in what is called the "bran," and the inside of the seed is called the "germ." Although we tend to think of grains as just seeds, they are fruits, as they come from ripened ovaries. Plants that produce grains are the most important food-producing plants in the world. Corn and wheat are examples of grains. Each ear of corn or stalk of wheat contains many grains.

Pods or legumes: Pods always have a row of seeds attached to the side of the fruit. They usually split open along both sides when the seeds are ready. Pea plants, peanut plants, and bean plants all produce pods.

Capsules: Capsules have several seeds inside. They split open when ready, revealing a group of seeds collected in one hardened ovary. They can split down the sides or around the middle. Some have "windows" that open at the top of the capsule, and the seeds fall out of those "windows." The fruits of the poppy and primrose plants are capsules.

Follicle: A follicle is a lot like a capsule, but it splits open along only one side when it releases its seed or seeds. Magnolia trees produce fruits that have one seed in each follicle, while milkweed plants produce fruits in which many seeds are in one follicle.

Achene (uh keen'): An achene is a single seed inside a shell, but the seed must be separated from the shell. A grain is also a single seed in a shell, but in a grain, the seed is attached to the shell. In an achene, it is not. Achenes usually form in groups. They can have parachutes attached, like dandelion seeds, or they can have hard shells, like sunflower seeds.   The strawberry plant produces many achenes on each fruit.

Samaras: Samaras are seeds inside a winged fruit that floats in the breeze. Samaras that are attached to one another making a two-winged fruit are called schizocarps. The samara is also a kind of achene, since it's only one seed inside a single shell. Maple, ash, and elm trees produce samaras.

Nuts: A single seed surrounded by a hard, woody covering is called a nut. Nuts float in water and are often buried by squirrels. They are also harvested by humans in orchards. Acorns and chestnuts are examples of nuts. A peanut is not really a nut, because it usually contains more than one seed.

Notebook Activities

Take out five sheets of paper. Title them "Human-Dispersed," "Wind-Dispersed," "Water-Dispersed," "Mechanically-Dispersed," and "Animal-Dispersed." On each sheet, write down descriptions or illustrate pictures of each of these kinds of seed dispersion.

A Nutty Game

Make a game that you can play with your family to help remember the different kinds of fruits and the way they are dispersed. Since a lot of seeds are dispersed by humans, we will leave human dispersal out to make the game a little harder.

You will need:
♦ A file folder to serve as the game board
♦ Index cards
♦ Colored pencils
♦ Different nuts or pods to use as game pieces (peanut, walnut, pecan, acorn, for example)
♦ A six-sided die

Game Preparation

Note to the teacher: The names "Tooty Fruity" and "Going Nuts" may not suit everyone. Feel free to make up your own names for this game. Other names might be: Fruit Loops, Fruit Shoot, Nuts and Stuff, or any other fun name you can imagine. To help with the fruit card gathering, you may be able to find cards with different fruits and vegetables listed on them in the produce section of your grocery store. If you did not cover the material in the "Fruit Types" section, you may not want to do this activity.

1. Begin by drawing (or pasting) pictures of a different fruit on each index card. At the bottom of the card, in small letters, write down what kind of fruit it is (pome, drupe, etc.) and how it is dispersed. You will lay the cards face down on the game board.
2. Open the file folder so that it lays flat on a table. This will be your game board.
3. Draw a rectangle for the cards near the center of the board.
4. Draw a line from one end of the board to the other, and then draw another line next to it, making a trail. You can make the trail so that it curves through the game board, or you can make it go around the edges of the game board like the trail in a Monopoly® game board.

5. Between the two lines that make up the trail, draw intersecting lines so that the trail looks like it is made up of squares. These squares will be the spaces for the game pieces.
6. Write "Start" on the first square, and write "Finish" on the last. Next, pick out a few of the spaces on different parts of the trail, and write "Going Nuts!" in them. If players land on these spaces, something bad happens to them.
7. On each "Going Nuts!" space, write down a different negative consequence. For example: "Go back to the beginning and start over" (you might put this one near the beginning so as to not discourage young players); "Go back two spaces;" "Move everyone except yourself forward one space." Make sure each "Going Nuts!" space has a different instruction on it.
8. Every third square or so, draw a picture of a piece of fruit smiling and label it "Tooty Fruity!" Color the rest of the squares in with different colors.
9. You can decorate the rest of the game board as you like, using stickers, drawings, or pictures that you cut out of magazines or newspapers. Write the name of the game on the game board.

To Play

1. Stack the cards face down in the rectangle that you drew for them.
2. Begin with all of the pieces (the pods and nuts) on the square labeled "Start."
3. The youngest player begins by rolling the die.

4. If the player's piece lands on a colored space, another player will pick up the card on the top of the deck, cover up the answers at the bottom, and show him the fruit. The player then has to tell everyone the fruit type and how it is dispersed. For example, if the card has a dandelion tuft on it, he should say, "That is an achene, which is dispersed by the wind." If he gets the name of the kind of fruit right, he gets to go again. If he gets the way it is dispersed right, he gets to move up to the next "Tooty Fruity" space. If both answers are correct, he gets move forward to the next "Tooty Fruity" space and then he gets to go again. If he misses both, go to the next player.

5. If anyone lands on a "Going Nuts" space, he must follow the instructions written on the space and wait until his next turn to go again.

If you would like to be really creative, design your own game that will help you remember fruits and how they are dispersed!

Project

Split a Squash

Spiritual Application - Planting Seeds

In the Bible, Jesus tells a story that says sharing the good news about Him is like planting seeds (Matt 13:3-8). Why do you think Jesus told this story? How can it be that if I tell my neighbor about Jesus, I am planting seeds?

You will need:
- A squash or medium-sized pumpkin
- An adult with a sharp knife

1. Cut your pumpkin or squash in half.
2. Count how many seeds are inside. Isn't it simply amazing how many seeds this one fruit from one vine can produce?

How many seeds do you think it took to grow this one fruit? You might be surprised to learn that a single seed produces many fruits, because a single pumpkin or squash seed produces a single vine, and a single vine might have several fruits. Each one of those fruits will have about as many seeds as the one you cut open. Let's suppose the vine from which your fruit came had a total of 20 fruits on it. How many total seeds, then, did this one seed produce? To answer that question, multiply the number of seeds you counted by 20. Each one of the seeds in your fruit could produce roughly the same number of seeds. Now, if you count all the seeds the one seed that was planted to grow this one vine produced, and then you count all the seeds those seeds could produce, how many seeds in all could that one seed make? To answer that question, multiply the number you just got by itself. That's a lot of seeds, isn't it? Of course, the number of seeds produced by that single seed will increase as each seed grows into a new plant that produces more seeds. Can you see how sharing Jesus with one person can be like the one seed that grew your pumpkin? Explain in your own words how sharing Jesus is like planting seeds.

Do you think every single seed that a plant produces will grow into a new plant? No, not every one will. The same is true when it comes to sharing Christ with others. Sometimes, you will share Christ with others, and it won't matter to them. Nevertheless, we should still continue to plant seeds, because some of them will certainly grow and produce more seeds that will be planted to grow and produce more and more and more. One day, when you get to heaven, you will be able to see all the work that was done through you because you were faithful to plant the one seed that was needed.

How do we plant seeds? Here are some practical suggestions, but remember that God will lead you in specific situations if you ask Him. You can plant seeds by asking people what they think about Jesus and then telling them what Jesus means to you. You can tell them about the prayers He has answered and how He has helped you. When God answers a prayer, tell everyone you see about it. When people tell you they are worried or sad, ask them if you can pray with them. Pray diligently for everyone who needs it. You may not know how many seeds grew from the words you spoke to others, but God knows and is delighted with the things you do for Him.

Project
Which Flies Farthest?

In this experiment, you will determine which flies farther in the wind: a dandelion tuft or a samara. Make a hypothesis about which will fly farther. Use a Scientific Speculation Sheet to record your hypothesis.   If you enjoy this experiment, find other wind-dispersed seeds to test.

You will need:
- A dandelion tuft
- A samara
- A piece of paper
- A measuring device such as measuring tape or a ruler

1. Fold the paper accordion-style to make a fan.
2. Place both fruits on a table. Fan them with one stroke of the fan.
3. Measure the distance each fruit traveled when it was fanned. Record the distances.
4. After you have done this several times, look at your numbers and determine which fruit consistently traveled the farthest. Was your hypothesis correct?

Lesson 6
Leaves

Did you know that most plants have a mouth? Believe it or not, they have several mouths.
Yes, they have many, many tiny mouths, but you probably haven't seen these little mouths, because
they are microscopic (my' kroh skop' ik). That means
they are too small to see with just your eyes. Even
though you can't see them with just your eyes, you can
see them with the help of a microscope (my' kroh skohp).
The drawings on the right show you what these little
mouths look like when you see them with the help of a
microscope. Do you know where the mouths are? Can
you guess? I'm sure you know that this lesson is about
leaves, so you probably guessed that they are on the
leaves! You are right! On the bottom side of every leaf
are many little mouths, called **stomata** (stoh mah' tah).
Stoma (stoh' muh) is a Greek word that means **mouth**.
Because of this, one mouth on a leaf is called a stoma,
and more than one are called stomata.

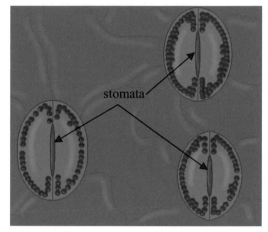

This drawing shows you what closed stomata
on a leaf look like under a microscope.

Do you need your mouth to live? Your mouth is as important to your body as the plants'
mouths are to them. These stomata are tiny, but they open and close just like your mouth. These little
leaf mouths don't eat food the way our mouths do, but
they actually help the leaf *make food for the plant*.
Remember that most of the living things in God's
creation eat (consume) plants or other creatures. As a
result, they are called **consumers**. Plants, on the other
hand, are quite special, because they can make
(produce) their own food. This is why we call plants
producers. In this lesson, we are going to learn more
about the interesting process by which plants make
their own food.

Leaves are the food factories of plants.

Stomata help the plant make its food by allowing important chemicals in the air to come into
the leaf. Without stomata in its leaves, a plant would not be able to live. Of course, since the stomata
are in the plant's leaves, the plant must also have leaves in order to live. When you start collecting
leaves for this course, then, be careful. Take only one leaf from each plant so that the plant will still be
able to live!

As I told you before, if you look at the underside of a leaf with a good microscope, you will see something like the drawing that is on the top of the previous page. The stomata are tiny holes in the leaf. They are surrounded by little structures called **guard cells**. Do you know what a cell is? The cell is the basic building block of life. All living things are made up of at least one cell. You can think of cells as tiny "bricks" that are used to "build" a living creature. If a person put bricks together in a certain arrangement, he can make a house. In the same way, when God puts cells together in a certain arrangement, He makes living things.

guard cells

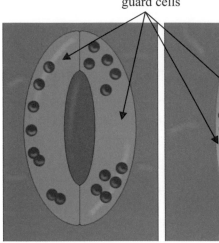

Now let's talk about guard cells. Each stoma is surrounded by two banana-shaped guard cells, as drawn on the right. When the guard cells expand, they bow outwards, away from each other. That opens the stoma. Look at the left side of the drawing. The cells are larger on that side of the drawing, and notice how there is a large hole in between them. The hole is the stoma. When the guard cells shrink, they end up nestling closer together, which closes the stoma. Look at the right side of the drawing. The cells are smaller there, and notice that the hole is nearly gone.

When the guard cells expand, the stoma gets large. That means it is open.

When the guard cells shrink, the stoma gets very small. That means it is closed.

As soon as the sun rises in the morning, the guard cells swell, and the stomata open. This allows a chemical in the air, called **carbon** (kar' bun) **dioxide** (dye ox' eyed), into the leaf. The leaf then uses that carbon dioxide to make food for the plant. You'll learn more about how the leaf does this in the next section. When the sun sets, the guard cells shrink. This closes the stomata, and carbon dioxide no longer gets into the leaf. At that point, the leaf takes a break from the hard work of making food for the plant. Why does the leaf "rest" like this at night? You'll learn about that in a little while.

The stomata do a lot of work for the plant, don't they? I bet you had no idea that leaves were that important to the plant! When I was a child, my mother had beautiful fern plants lining the entry hall of our home. Every day as I passed by, I would grab one branch of leaves and, beginning at the bottom, pull my fingers up the branch, enjoying the sensation of every leaf popping off. I didn't know that the leaves were so important to the survival of the plant and that I was making the plant weaker and weaker as I removed its tiny little mouths each day.

Leaves are necessary in order for this fern to live.

Not only are a plant's leaves important for its survival, they are important for your survival as well. Yes indeed! Plants not only provide food for us to eat, they also release **oxygen** into the air for us to breathe! This is something else the stomata do: They allow oxygen to leave the leaves so that we can breathe it. Without the leaves that surround us on this earth, there would be less oxygen for you and me to breathe. That would be very bad for us, since we need oxygen to survive. In fact, the reason that we breathe is so that our bodies can get oxygen from the air. Without plants, it would be much harder for us to get the oxygen that we need!

Believe it or not, plants also clean the air! When I pulled the leaves off the ferns in my mother's house, I was not only removing their food source, I was also removing our household air

Plants reduce the amount of pollution in the air by absorbing some of the pollutants.

purifiers! Plants clean the air by taking in carbon dioxide and replacing it with oxygen. They also absorb harmful chemicals that are dangerous for us to inhale. Because plants absorb those chemicals, you and I do not breathe them. Instead, we breathe the wonderful oxygen that the plants make for us! What a great idea God had when He created plants to work this way. He made plants to bless humans in such amazing ways! Can you see how the more plants you have in your house, the better and cleaner the air will be? It would be good to have a living plant in every room. Maybe you could take the responsibility to water all of the plants in your home. It would be worth the work in order to have nice clean air to breathe!

What Do You Remember?

Why are the leaves of a plant so important? Can you explain to someone what the stomata do for a plant? Explain what would happen if a plant lost all its leaves. What does a plant take in from the air and what does it put back into the air?

Photosynthesis

Making food is a big job for a plant. It takes a lot of complicated steps. Do you remember what kind of food plants like to eat? It starts with an "s" and is one of your favorite foods, too. Plants and children (and adults) love sugar. Without sugar, plants would die. Where do you think the sugar is made? Take a guess! Sugar is made right inside the leaf! The leaf takes water from the roots and combines it with light from the sun and the carbon dioxide from the air to make sugar for the plant and oxygen for all the rest of God's creation. It then sends that sugar down from the leaves, and the sugar runs throughout the entire plant to feed it.

Have you ever broken the stem of plant to find that liquid gooey stuff dripped out? That liquid gooey stuff is **sap**, a mixture of water, sugar, and other chemicals that travel throughout the plant. Some plants, like the maple tree, have sap that we can eat, but some plants have sap that is poisonous for us. The sappy plant food gives the plant energy to make more leaves, to grow taller and stronger, and to make flowers. We know how important flowers are to a plant, don't we?

Do you like maple syrup on your pancakes? If you do, then thank God for creating maple trees, because you are using their sap to make your pancakes taste better! That's right. Maple syrup comes from the sap of the maple tree. However, *real* maple syrup is more expensive than the brand-name pancake syrups that line the grocery store shelves. That's because getting real maple syrup is not easy! Most brand-name syrups are just sugar water with pretend maple flavor. Getting real maple syrup takes time.

In the early spring, maple tree farmers poke holes into maple trees and place faucets in the holes. They then put buckets beneath the faucets. As the sap runs through the trees, some of it flows out of the faucets and into the buckets. The farmers then boil the sap and bottle it to send across the nation for people to buy and pour on their pancakes. Genuine maple syrup is very special because all of this must happen quickly. The sap is only tasty and sweet for about 2-8 weeks. As a result, all of the sap used to make real maple syrup is collected in just 2-8 weeks out of each year.

The buckets on these maple trees are collecting sap which will be made into real maple syrup.

So how do the leaves make this sappy plant food? Well, the process is called **photosynthesis** (foh' toh sin' thuh sis), and it is truly amazing. Each leaf is like a little sugar-making factory. When its stomata open, it starts taking in carbon dioxide. At the same time, water travels up from the roots of the plants to the leaves, and the leaf actually takes the carbon dioxide and combines it with the water. Guess what that makes? It makes sugar and oxygen. The leaf uses some of the sugar for food, sends the rest of it down to the rest of the plant, and releases the oxygen into the air for you and me to breathe.

Well, it turns out that the leaf can't actually do this job on its own. In order to combine the carbon dioxide and water, the leaf needs energy. Guess where it gets that energy? It gets it from light! That's the "photo" part of "photosynthesis." You see, **photo** means **light**, and **synthesis** means **to put**

together. So "photosynthesis" means "putting together with light." That's exactly what leaves do. With the help of light, they put together carbon dioxide and water to make sugar and oxygen.

Now do you see why a leaf's stomata close at night? The stomata's job is to take in carbon dioxide and release oxygen. Well, at night, there is no light for photosynthesis. As a result, the leaves can no longer make sugar and oxygen. Well, if they can't make sugar and oxygen, they don't need carbon dioxide, so the stomata close, allowing to leaves to rest. This is good, because the leaves need their rest! They start working as soon as the sun rises, and they work nonstop, seven days a week, until the sun goes down. All of that time, they are making sugar for the plant and oxygen for the rest of God's creation!

Color-Fill

Have you ever wondered why leaves are green? Flowers come in many colors, but leaves are green. Why? The answer is that they *need to be green* in order to do their job. Remember, leaves need light in order to make food for the plant. How do they use this light? Well, leaves are filled with a special substance called **chlorophyll** (klor' uh fill), which absorbs the light that the leaves need in order to do their job. It takes the light's energy and gives it to the leaf in just the right way so that the leaf can use it. This chlorophyll makes the leaves green. We can remember this because "chlor" sounds sort of like color, and "phyll" sounds like "fill." So chlorophyll fills the leaves with green color. Since chlorophyll is necessary in order for a leaf to use light for photosynthesis, you know that if a leaf is green, it can do photosynthesis. If a leaf is not green (in the fall, for example), it cannot do photosynthesis.

Photosynthesis requires light, chlorophyll (which makes leaves green), carbon dioxide from the air, and water from the soil.

Have you ever left a board or something like that on the grass during the summer? In a day or two, when you picked the board back up, the grass underneath wasn't green anymore, was it? It was still alive, but it was a pale yellow color. Why? Well, the board blocked the sunlight from the grass, so the grass could no longer do photosynthesis. This means its chlorophyll was not being used, so it decayed away. The green color of the grass decayed away with the chlorophyll. What happened after you picked the board up? In just a few days, the grass regained its nice green color, didn't it? That's because picking the board up allowed sunlight to start hitting the grass again, and the grass started making chlorophyll so that it could use the sunlight for photosynthesis.

Think about the project that you did in Lesson 2. You grew seedlings in a window, in a dark closet, and in a refrigerator. Did you notice that the seedling that grew in the closet grew longer and taller than the other plants? It grew longer and taller because it was using all the stored food in the cotyledon to try to find a way out of the darkness and into the light. Did you notice that it was paler in color than the plant next to the window? That's because it was not making much chlorophyll, because without light, it could not do photosynthesis.

When a plant makes sugar through photosynthesis, it uses some of the sugar right away and stores the rest for later. Different plants store their food differently. Often, a plant will store its extra food in "lumps" that are in the stems or the roots. A carrot plant, for example, stores its extra food in a lump in its root. We call that lump the "carrot," and that's what we eat. A potato plant actually stores its extra food in an underground stem that we call a "tuber." What you call a potato, then, is just a special underground stem in which the plant's extra food has been stored. Do you see how God takes care of us and the other consumers in creation? He designed plants to make more food than they need. That way, they store their excess food so that consumers can eat it! It is amazing how God created plants to do this.

What Do You Remember?

Can you explain photosynthesis in your own words? Can you remember the four things a plant needs to make food? What kind of food does the plant make?   What happens when one ingredient is removed? What makes leaves green?

Notebook Activities

Make an illustration page for this lesson in your notebook. It should illustrate that a plant needs light, water, chlorophyll, and carbon dioxide in order to make food for itself. Make another illustration showing the stomata of a leaf. Write down (or dictate to your parent) what the stomata do.

Testing a Hypothesis

Did you know that not everything you read in science books is true? That's right. Science books sometimes have mistakes in them. Even as a young student, you can devise (that means make up) tests that will help you determine whether statements made in a science book are true or false. Let's try to do that now. In this book, you learned about four things that a plant needs in order to do photosynthesis. I want you to figure out an experiment that will test whether or not this is true for at least two of those things: sunlight and water. What do you think is the best way to test the scientific belief that plants need water and sunlight to do photosynthesis? Think about that for a moment before you move on. What could you do to see if that is true?

To test this idea, you could do an experiment with a plant that has one of these ingredients removed and see what happens. For example, suppose you put a plant in total darkness and it died. Would that demonstrate that plants need light to live? Believe it or not, it wouldn't really demonstrate that. It might just demonstrate that you do not know how to take care of a plant. Perhaps the plant would have also died even if you gave it light, because you are just a bad gardener. How, then, can we test to see if a plant needs light to live?

Well, suppose you did a slightly different experiment. Suppose you took two plants of the same type and put one in total darkness and left the other in the light. Suppose that you took care of both plants in exactly the same way. That way, the only difference between the two plants is that one was given light and the other wasn't. If the plant that got light lived while the other one died, *that* would be a good indication that plants need light to survive. In this kind of experiment, the plant that got light is called the **control** of the experiment. It is the "standard" plant, and the only thing different between it and the test plant is light. The presence or absence of light is called the **variable** of the experiment, because it is what varied between the control and the rest of the experiment. In a good experiment, there is always a control, and there is only one variable for each subject in the experiment. That way, the difference between the control and the subject is most likely due to the variable.

Now it is time for you to design and perform an experiment that tests whether or not a plant needs water or light in order to grow. First, choose your variable: light or water. Once you have chosen, decide how the test plant will differ from the control plant. How will you keep water from the test plant? How will you keep light from the test plant? This activity may take a few days, but it will be your own experiment that you made up yourself! Remember to use a Scientific Speculation Sheet to record all that you did.

Transpiration

Do you remember what the stomata do? They take in the carbon dioxide from the air for photosynthesis. They also release oxygen from the leaves. Well, that's not all they do! They also have another important job. The stomata also release excess water from the plant that comes up from the roots. This is called **transpiration** (tran spuh ray' shun).

All day long, the roots of the plant absorb water from the soil. They then send the water through the plant's veins to the leaves. The leaves, in turn, use the water for photosynthesis. It turns

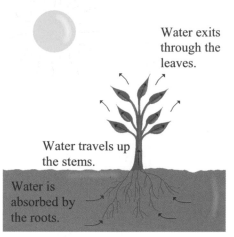

Water exits through the leaves.

Water travels up the stems.

Water is absorbed by the roots.

Transpiration causes a plant to lose water.

out, however, that the roots send up more water than is needed for photosynthesis, so the left-over water is pushed out of the plant through the stomata. That's transpiration. As long as the plant is doing photosynthesis, then, it is also transpiring, because it must get rid of the excess water.

One of the best places to study transpiration is in a rainforest. The rainforests in Africa and South America, for example, are filled with many amazingly large plants that have gigantic leaves. The leaves grow large to better capture the very few rays of sunlight that peek through the dense trees of the forest. Because there is so much rain in the rainforests, the plants have a lot of opportunities to transpire. They suck up the rain water and release it through their leaves in large quantities each day. Because the leaves are so large, this fills the air with water, making it moist. When there is a lot of moisture in the air, it becomes very humid.

The rainforest is a very humid place partly because of transpiration. There is so much water in the air that if a seed lands on a tree, it can begin growing right there on the tree because it has all the water it needs to germinate and keep growing!

Leaves of rainforest plants are often very large.

Falling Leaves

Many trees lose their leaves in the winter to conserve water.

Without leaves, plants can't make the sugar that they need to survive. What would happen to the plants in your yard if you pulled off all their leaves? They would probably die, unless they had enough sugar stored inside of them to survive long enough to make more leaves. In the winter, some plants shed their leaves and live off the sugar they stored up during the spring and summer.

Transpiration is actually the reason that these plants lose their leaves in autumn. You see, God designed some plants to lose their leaves as a way to protect the plant during the frozen, dry winter. Because rain is scarce and often water is frozen in the winter, it is difficult for the roots to get enough water for the plant or tree. Remember what happens in transpiration. Water escapes the plant through its leaves. What if the plant continued the lose water through the leaves all winter, even though it couldn't replace it with water from the roots? The plant would die of thirst!

Well, God has designed many trees and plants to avoid this problem by losing their leaves in the fall, before winter sets in. These plants are called **deciduous** (duh sid' you us) plants. They lose their leaves so that they will not lose anymore water through transpiration. They have enough water and stored sugar inside their roots and stems to keep them until spring, so they don't need their leaves to make more food. As a result, they lose their leaves in order to save water.

How does a plant lose its leaves? The place where the leaf is connected to the tree is called the **petiole** (peh' tee ohl). In the fall, deciduous plants form a little scab between the tree branch and the petiole. Because it has been cut off by the scab growth, the leaf can no longer get water from the tree. What happens to a leaf if

The red in this leaf was always there. As the chlorophyll decays, the red begins to show through.

it can't get water? It quits doing photosynthesis, and it no longer makes chlorophyll. Because it no longer makes chlorophyll, the leaf begins to lose its green color. When this happens, the leaf begins to show all of the colors that were already there, hidden under all the green chlorophyll. In the fall, then, a leaf doesn't turn red, it already was red! The green chlorophyll was so dark, however, that all spring and summer it covered up the other colors that were already there. As the chlorophyll decays away and is not replaced by new chlorophyll, the beautiful colors that the chlorophyll was hiding show up.

Leaves fall in the autumn as the connection between the tree and the petiole weakens.

As the chlorophyll in the leaf decays away, the connection between the petiole and the tree gets weaker and weaker. Pretty soon, it is so weak that when the wind blows, the leaf falls off the tree. This tells us that winter is on its way.

Explain transpiration in your own words. Explain why some trees lose their leaves in the fall and how the plant survives the winter without its leaves. Be sure to use the scientific name for these plants.

Project
Testing Transpiration

You can conduct a little experiment to actually "see" transpiration occurring in a plant.

You will need:
- ♦ A plastic sandwich bag
- ♦ A clothespin
- ♦ A living plant that is not an evergreen

1. Wrap the plastic bag around one leaf (preferably a broad, flat one) of a living plant in your home.
2. Seal the bag at the petiole (the little stalk that attaches the bottom of the leaf to the stem of the plant – see drawing below) with a clothespin.
3. Water the plant.
4. Observe the plastic bag several times a day for the next few days.
5. What do you think will happen? How long do you think it will take before you see results? Use a Scientific Speculation Sheet to record your experiment, your hypothesis, and the results.

Anatomy of a Leaf

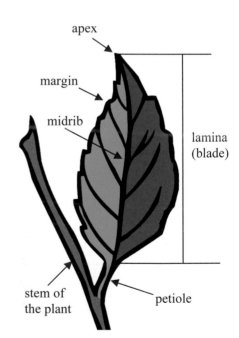

When we study **anatomy**, we are studying the individual parts that make up a larger body. For example, all the different parts of a leaf make up the leaf's anatomy. The drawing on the right shows you the basic anatomy of a simple leaf.

The very tip of the leaf is called the **apex** of the leaf. The petiole is the "stalk" that attaches the leaf to the plant, and the **midrib** is the main vein of the leaf. It is actually an extension of the petiole, and it runs most of the length of the leaf. If the leaf has branching veins, the other veins start at the midrib. The entire leaf above the petiole is the called the **lamina** (lam' ih nuh) or blade, and the edge that surrounds the leaf is called the **margin**.

Now that you have learned the basic anatomy of a leaf, find a leaf and see if you can name the parts without looking at the drawing. Why is it important to learn the anatomy of a leaf? Well, different plants have leaves with different types of margins, veins, etc. If we can learn the different kinds of leaf parts in creation, we can begin to learn how to identify plants based on their leaves.

Simple Leaves and Compound Leaves

Leaves are often put into two main groups based on how they are attached to the plant. A **simple leaf** is one leaf attached to the stem of the plant by a single petiole. A **compound leaf** has several leaflets attached to a single petiole. We call such leaves compound leaves because **compound** means **more than one**.

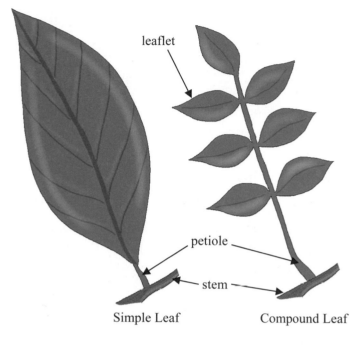

The drawing on the right illustrates the difference between simple and compound leaves. Although the compound leaf may look like a stem with several leaves on it, it is not. The stem of the plant is shown on the bottom, and a single petiole connects the entire compound leaf to the plant. The individual blades on a compound leaf are usually called **leaflets**.

It may take some time for you to get used to recognizing compound leaves, but the key is to be able to determine where the petiole attaches to the plant. If you can determine where the petiole is, you can then see if it leads to only one leaf (which means the leaf is a simple leaf) or many leaflets (which means the leaf is a compound leaf). The pictures below show you compound leaves so that you can get used to identifying them.

These plants both have compound leaves. On the left, the leaflets all come out of a central petiole. On the right, a single petiole attaches to the plant's stem, and the leaflets emerge from that petiole.

Leaf Arrangement

The arrangement of leaves on the stem often helps to identify a plant. There are three basic arrangements for leaves: **opposite**, **alternate**, and **whorled**. Leaves that are directly opposite one another going up the stem have opposite arrangement. Leaves that are not directly across from one another on the stem, but alternate as you travel up the stem, have alternate arrangement. Finally, leaves that are attached to the stem and arranged in a ring around the stem have the whorled arrangement. Drawings of simple leaves in each of the three arrangements are shown below.

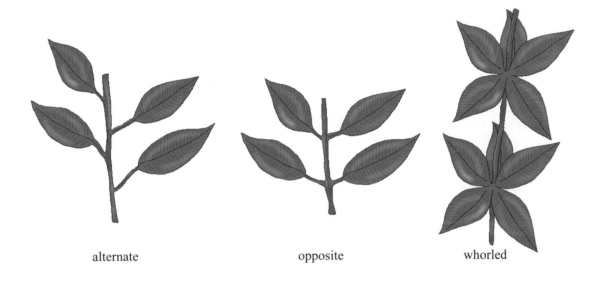

alternate   opposite   whorled

To give you an idea of what these arrangements look like in real life, here are some photographs of plants with each of these leaf arrangements.

These are compound leaves in an alternate arrangement on the stem.

These are simple leaves in an opposite arrangement on the stem.

These are simple leaves in a whorled arrangement on the stem.

Leaf Venation

As you have already learned, the pattern of veins on a leaf, which we call the leaf's **venation** (ven ay' shun), can tell you a lot about a plant. You learned in Lesson 2 that monocots produce leaves with veins that do not branch, while dicots produce leaves with veins that branch. Well, when a leaf's veins run up and down the leaf without intersecting, we say that it has **parallel venation**. When a leave's veins all branch out from a single vein in the middle (the midrib), we say that the leaf has **pinnate venation**. Finally, when a leave's veins not only branch out from the midrib, but those branches also have branches on them, the leaf has **palmate venation**. These three types of venation are illustrated below.

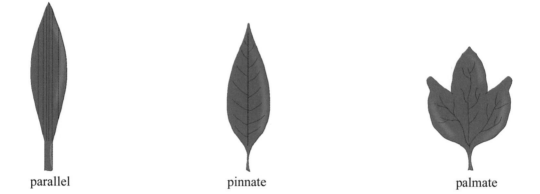

parallel   pinnate   palmate

Now remember, monocots produce leaves whose veins don't branch. This means that monocots have leaves with parallel venation. The leaves of dicots, however, have veins that branch. As a result, dicot leaves can have either pinnate or palmate venation.

Leaf Shapes

As you already know, God created His world with a lot of variety. You have already seen that plants produce many different kinds of flowers, fruits, and seeds. It's not surprising, then, that they also produce a wide variety of leaves. In this section of the course, I want to go through the different kinds of leaf shapes that we see in creation. This is not a complete list, but it does cover most of the leaf shapes that you will see in nature.

Before I go through these shapes, it is important for you to understand that I am giving you this material for reference. In other words, when you need to determine the shape of a leaf, you can come back to this part of the book and look it up. In the leaf classification activity near the end of this lesson, for example, you can come back to these pages to compare the leaves you find with the drawings that are here. This will help you to identify the shapes of the leaves that you find in the activity.

Many leaves in creation are a lot longer than they are wide. Sometimes, the leaves are **linear**, which means that they are about the same width from the top of the leaf to the bottom. If the leaf is wider at the bottom (near the petiole) and tapers towards the top (the apex), we say that it has a **lanceolate** (lan' see uh late) shape. The upside-down version of the lanceolate shape is the **oblanceolate** (ob' lan' see uh late) shape. In this shape, the leaf is broader at the apex and tapers down to the petiole. If the leaf tapers at both the petiole and the apex, but is still longer than it is wide, it has an **elliptical** (ee lip' tik uhl) shape. If, on the other hand, there is no tapering on either end, and the leaf is about twice as long as it is wide, we say that the leaf has an **oblong** shape.

linear   lanceolate   oblanceolate   elliptical   oblong

Although many leaves are a lot longer than they are wide, there are some that are more "egg-shaped." In other words, they are only a bit longer than they are wide. If a leaf is egg-shaped, we call say that it has an **oval** shape. If it is shaped a little like an egg but tapers towards the apex, its shape is called **ovate**. Now don't get confused between ovate and lanceolate. Both of them are wide at the bottom and taper towards the top, but a laceolate leaf is a *lot* longer than it is wide, while an ovate leaf is only a little longer than it is wide. The upside-down version of the ovate shape is the **obovate** (ah boh' vayt) shape, which is egg-shaped but tapers towards the petiole. Finally, if the leaf is somewhat egg-shaped but the taper towards the petiole is very long, the leaf shape is **spatulate** (spat' you late), which means **spoon-shaped**.

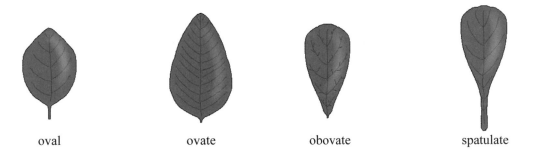

oval   ovate   obovate   spatulate

Some leaves have shapes that are very familiar to us. They often look like triangles, circles, or hearts. A leaf that is triangular in shape is called a **deltoid** (del' toyd) leaf. If it looks like an upside-down heart, it is a **cordate** (kor' dayt) leaf. If it looks a bit like an upside-down heart but is much wider and more circular, it is a **reniform** (which means **kidney-shaped**) leaf. If it is shaped more like a wedge, it is a **cuneate** (kyou' nee ate) leaf. If the leaf is nearly circular, we call its shape **orbicular** (or bik' you lur), which means circular.

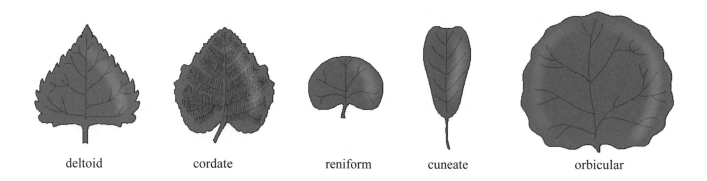

deltoid	cordate	reniform	cuneate	orbicular

Finally, there are some leaf shapes that are more irregular than the ones I have discussed so far. For example, there are **lobed** leaves that have deep indentations in the leaf. If the indentations are very deep and tend to be sharp, the leaf has a **clef** shape. The needles on pine trees are actually leaves, and although they are linear, we usually give them their own shape, calling them **needle-like** leaves. Some trees have leaves that look a bit like needles, but they are not as long as needles and look almost like thin triangles. We say that these are **awl-like** leaves. Finally, some plants have leaves that look almost like the scales on a fish. Not surprisingly, they are called **scale-like** leaves.

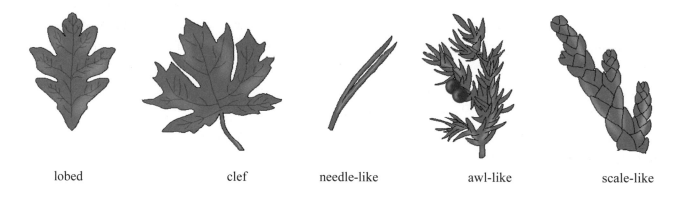

lobed	clef	needle-like	awl-like	scale-like

Now please remember that these are not the only leaf shapes in creation. However, they do represent most of what you will see when you are looking at leaves.

Leaf Margins

Do you remember what the margin of a leaf is? It is the outer edge of the leaf. Well, it turns out that there are also many different margins that a leaf can have. If the outer edge of a leaf is smooth with no indentations or teeth, it has an **entire** margin. If, on the other hand, the leaf has tiny, sharp teeth along its outer edge, it has a **serrate** (seh' rate) margin. With serrate margins, the teeth usually point upwards towards the apex of the leaf. If a leaf's outer edge has more pronounced teeth that also point outward rather than just towards the apex, it has a **dentate** margin. If the teeth are rounded rather than pointed, the margin is called **crenate** (kree' nate). Finally, if the leaf's edge doesn't have teeth but tends to be wavy, we say that it has an **undulate** (un' joo late) margin.

entire   serrate   dentate   crenate   undulate

Now the real trick to identifying leaves is to try to determine the venation, shape, and margin all at the same time. You will have plenty of opportunity to try this yourself when you do the second notebook activity described in the next section. However, I want you to see how this is done by showing you a few examples.

These are elliptical leaves (they taper at both ends and are a lot longer than they are wide) with entire (smooth) margins.

These are lanceolate leaves (they taper significantly at the apex) with serrate (jagged) margins.

These are cordate (heart-shaped) leaves with dentate (pronounced teeth that also point outwards rather than just towards the apex) margins.

These are linear leaves with entire margins. They taper a bit, but they are so much longer than they are wide that they are considered linear.

Notebook Activities
The Anatomy of a Leaf

Draw a leaf for your notebook, labeling all of the parts of the anatomy. You can use the drawing on page 96 as a guide. Also, make a drawing that illustrates the difference between a simple leaf and a compound leaf.

Leaf Classification

Now it's time to add some spice to your notebook. You are going to collect leaves, and then you will classify each leaf according to its arrangement on the plant, its venation, its shape, and its margin. If you are able, take some time to go outside and pick one of each kind of leaf that you can find. Remember, it is okay to collect leaves from plants, but be careful to take only what you need. If you cannot find many leaves outside, go to the grocery store and buy a mixed salad package. After you have collected the leaves, come back and look through information presented in the past few sections and see if  you can classify each leaf by arrangement, venation, shape, and margin. Of course, if you end up using the salad mix, you will not be able to classify the leaf by arrangement, because the leaves in a salad mix have been removed from the stems. Use a field guide to try to identify the plants from which your leaves came.

After you have gathered and identified your leaves, label each leaf and glue them onto the paper with white school glue. The glue will serve to preserve the green color. Allow the glue to dry before inserting the paper into your notebook. Organize your leaves however you think best.

Storybook Activity for Younger Students

I want you to make a storybook about the life of a leaf. You can write it yourself or dictate it to your parent / teacher so that she can write it down. Give your leaf a personality and a name. Start your story with the leaf beginning its life in the spring, going through the warm summer, and eventually falling off the tree to join his friends on the ground. Make sure you include the fact that the leaf works very hard making food for the plant. Mention how its tiny "mouths" take in carbon dioxide and let out oxygen. Does the leaf enjoy this hard work, or does the leaf resent it? Does the leaf like making oxygen for animals and people? When the leaf falls off the tree, does it enjoy being raked into a pile to be jumped on? Draw pictures for each phase of your leaf's life.

Term Project for Older Students

Today you will begin your second term project. You are going to make your own field guide for plants! It will take you the rest of the term to complete it, but don't worry. It will be a ton of fun and you will really enjoy the end product. I suggest you limit your field guide to the plants that are in your yard. If your yard is very small, perhaps you can expand your field to include other parts of your neighborhood. There are many people who make field guides as their career. They publish them and sell them to people like you and me who want to learn about nature. They had to get their start somewhere, and I bet it was by making a field guide of their own area first. That's what you are going to do.

In what format will you put your field guide? Will you do it on loose leaf paper and keep the papers in a folder to have bound when you are finished? Will you keep it in notebook form, like your botany notebook? Will you keep it in a spiral notebook and take great care to organize it before you begin? Will you use the computer to type your field guide information? Will you put it in a document on the computer and scan in all your pictures? Will you use colored pencils (strongly encouraged) or will you use another means (like photographs) to illustrate the plants for your field guide?

The best way to plan your field guide is by checking out a few field guides from the library to see how they are formatted. What sections are they broken it into? What are the titles of the different chapters? What information do they include? What specific things about each plant do the drawings or photographs illustrate? What do you like about each guide? What do you dislike? What would you do similarly, and what would you do differently? Is the field guide too wordy and uninteresting for the average person? Is there not enough information about each plant to satisfy natural curiosity? Would this field guide be fun to read? Will yours be fun to read?

Whatever format you choose, do your very best work, as this field guide will be a very valuable and important book. Your family will enjoy having a resource that they can turn to when they want to know what kind of plant they are looking at in their yard. In other words, this will be an important book that can bless others.

Once you have decided what your field guide will look like and how it will be arranged, you need to spend some time deciding what kind of information you will include in it. The goal of the field guide will be to allow anyone to learn what kinds of plants grow in your yard (or neighborhood) and to be able to refer to the field guide to help identify a plant that is found in your yard. Here are some suggestions about what kind of information to include about each plant.

1. Is this plant a dicot or a monocot? How can you tell?
2. What color are its flowers? How many petals does the flower have? What color is the flower's carpel? How might the flower be pollinated? What does the fruit produced by the plant look like? How might its seeds be dispersed?
3. What is the shape of the leaf? How is it arranged on the plant? What does its margin look like? What is the texture of the leaf: rough, shiny, thick, furry? Does the plant lose its leaves or keep them throughout the winter?
4. How tall does the plant grow? Do you think it keeps getting bigger each year, or does it only grow to a certain height?
5. Does it completely die at the end of the year, or does it just lose its leaves?

Once you have decided what information to include about each plant, write down an outline of what you need to learn about each plant that you find. That way, you can make sure that you have collected all of the information that you need. I suggest that you keep a special notepad with you on all excursions outside to record this information.

When you begin illustrating your field guide, always make a rough sketch of the plant before you make your final drawing. You can then go back indoors with your notepad and transter the information with much care to your field guide. I know this sounds like a lot of work, but you have a long time to do it. If you just do a little bit every now and again, it won't be long before you have a very detailed, informative field guide!

Project
Make a Leaf Skeleton

Have you ever seen a leaf skeleton? A leaf skeleton is a leaf that has all the green "flesh" removed; all that is left are the veins that were hidden beneath. Sometimes you can find a leaf skeleton on the ground outside. You see, after leaves fall from a tree, their fleshy parts sometimes decay away, leaving the veins behind. This is nice, because it allows you to see the complete vein structure, parts of which are usually hidden by the green part of the leaf. If you have never found a leaf skeleton, don't worry. You are going to make your own by following the instructions below.

You will need:
♦ An adult
♦ A leaf or leaves
♦ A stove
♦ A pot for boiling
♦ Water
♦ 3 tablespoons of washing soda (You can find this in the laundry section of the grocery store.)
♦ Gloves (You need to wear gloves when you handle the washing soda. It is caustic.)
♦ A spatula
♦ Paper towels

1. Have an adult put on gloves and add 3 tablespoons of washing soda to the pot.
2. Have the adult add four cups of water and mix well.
3. Place the pot on the stove and heat it up until it starts to boil.
4. Once the water has been boiling for a few minutes, take the pot off the stove.
5. Add the leaves to the hot mixture in the pot. **Be careful! The water is very hot!**
6. Let the leaves sit in the hot mixture for about half an hour.
7. Using a spatula, remove the leaves from the pot.
8. A lot of the green part of the leaves should have come off in the mixture.
9. Gently rinse the leaf with water. Be careful not to break the veins.
10. The green stuff that remains on the leaf should feel slimy. Gently rub it off the leaf, being careful not to break the veins.
11. Let it dry.
12. Now you have a leaf skeleton to add to your notebook!

This is a leaf skeleton with just a bit of the "flesh" of the leaf still clinging to it.

Lesson 7
Roots

So far, we have been focusing our attention on the seed factories and sugar factories that you find above the ground in plants. Now let's dig below the surface to uncover the little water pipes beneath, which we call the **roots**. A plant's root system is really a network of tubes, usually growing underground, that branches out every which way. The roots have two main jobs: they absorb nutrients and water from the soil, and they hold the plant in place like an anchor.

Although roots are usually underground, parts of them sometimes stick out above ground.

Just like you and I, plants cannot live without water. The main way a plant gets water is through its roots. From the roots, the water goes up into the rest of the plant to be used in photosynthesis. Do you remember that photosynthesis is the process by which plants make their own food? The roots also absorb other things besides water. For example, the roots absorb valuable nutrients from the soil. The plant does not use these nutrients for food. It makes its own food. However, the plant does use the nutrients in other ways to keep itself healthy. You can think of these nutrients as "vitamins" for the plant. Just as vitamins help to keep you healthy, the nutrients that plants absorb from the soil can help to keep them healthy.

This hillside will not erode nearly as quickly as the mountains in the background, because the roots of the grass and flowers will anchor the dirt.

A plant's root system also acts like an anchor, keeping the plant from washing away with the rain or blowing away with the wind. An added benefit is that the roots also keep the soil from washing away. Rain and wind can whisk soil away, changing the landscape. This is called **erosion** (ee roh' shun). Roots help keep erosion from happening by clinging to the soil, holding it in place. If you are worried about a hillside or other area eroding away, you can help prevent the erosion by planting seeds. As the seeds grow into plants, the roots that the plants grow will hold the soil in place. So in fact, roots have three purposes in creation. They anchor the plant to the ground; they provide nutrients and water for the plant; and they help to prevent erosion.

Root Hairs

The hairs you see on these roots do most of the work of absorbing water and nutrients.

God covered the surface of roots with tiny hairs that look a lot like fur. You may remember seeing this furry-looking growth in some of your projects, especially the one in which you grew seeds inside of Ziploc® bags. The hairs appear soft and downy and seem a bit unimportant, but they are probably the most important part of a root! You see, these hairs are called **root hairs**, and they actually do most of the work of absorbing water and nutrients for the plant!

Each little root hair lives for about six weeks, working mightily throughout that time to serve the rest of the plant. It leads a very short but noble life! After about six weeks, new root hairs develop to take the place of the root hairs that wither away and die. The new root hairs then take over the job of drinking in water and nutrients for the plant. Without root hairs, a plant is likely to die.

When people transplant (that means move to another location) a plant in their yard, it often dies because too many of the root hairs were destroyed when the plant was moved. Most people do not realize that the most important parts of the roots are the root hairs. If enough root hairs are preserved when the plant is moved, the plant may be able to survive transplantation. Often, however, the plant will look like it is dying before it can revive itself. This is often called **transplant shock**. If you are careful to dig in a deep, wide circle around the plant, preserving the very tips of the roots and many root hairs, you can move a plant with little or no transplant shock.

Root Growth

Roots grow throughout the life of a plant. They grow longer from the tip, adding cells to the end of each root. Do you remember what cells are? They are the basic building blocks of life. You might think that a root grows by adding cells to the base of the root, but that's not right. Roots grow longer by adding cells to their tips, and they grow fatter by adding cells around their tube-like bodies.

Roots grow longer by adding cells to their tips, and they grow fatter by adding cells around their tube-like bodies.

To better understand how roots grow, think about building a tower out of Legos®. How would you do that? You would begin with the base of the tower, and then you would add Legos to the top of the tower, making it taller. You would probably also add Legos around the sides, making the tower wider. This is how roots grow as well. Interestingly enough, you and I don't grow this way. Our bodies add cells in order to make them grow, but the cells are added everywhere, in a very complex way.

At the tip of each root, there is a little group of tough cells called the root cap. The root cap is the strongest part of the root tip, and its job is to push its way through the dirt in search of moisture and nutrients. The root tip is so strong as it grows that it can push its way through cement and the concrete foundations upon which homes and buildings are laid. Tree roots can lift up whole houses over time! Have you ever walked along the sidewalk in an older neighborhood? Often, the sidewalks are full of cracks and are quite uneven. This is usually because of roots that grow underneath the sidewalk, shoving the cement out of the way. When you see an uneven sidewalk, it's probably the fault of a root somewhere down below.

Look at the picture on the right. It is a picture of a root tip, but the picture was taken through a microscope. This allows us to see things that are too small for us to see with our eyes alone. The squares and rectangles with little dots inside them are the cells of the root. The tiny root hairs are also pointed out, as is the area in which cells are being added to make the root grow longer. Notice how the root cap looks different from the rest of the root tip. That's because it is the strongest part of the root tip.

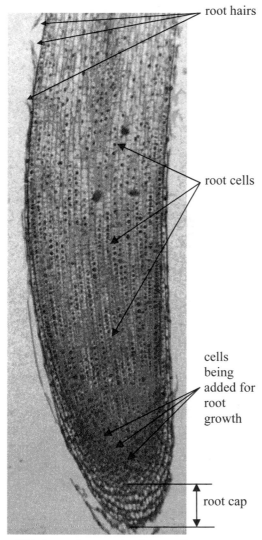

root hairs

root cells

cells being added for root growth

root cap

This is a microscopic picture of a root tip.

Roots can grow on and on and on. You may be digging in your yard one day and run into roots from a nearby tree. The tree might not be as near as you think, however. You see, roots can grow a long, long way in search of water and nutrients. A wild fig tree in South Africa, for example, grew roots that were more than 393 feet long! That's a *lot* of root growth!

Roots will grow on and on in their search for water and nutrients. If water and nutrients are present near the surface of the ground, they do not need to grow deep. Instead, they will grow outwards so that they can cover a larger area. They are greedy little things, too, for they will try to take over as much ground as possible in the hopes of soaking up all the water and nutrients that they can. If a dry spell suddenly occurs, or if the soil near the surface of the ground runs out of nutrients, the roots will then grow deep searching for what they need.

Do you remember that I said roots are usually found underground? Well, in some cases, that is not true. In the rainforest, a lot of water is present in the air. Do you remember why? In the previous lesson, you learned that the rainforest is full of plants with large leaves that are constantly doing transpiration. Because of the large amount of rain and the large amount of transpiration that occur in a rainforest, the air is very humid. This means it contains a lot of water. Because of this, you will often find rainforest plants growing right on trees, with roots hanging down into the air or running into the moss that is also growing on the trees. They don't even need the dirt;

Notice the fern and other plants growing on this tree. Their roots get all the water and nutrients they need from the air and from the moss that is also growing on the tree.

they have all they need floating around in the air or hidden away in the moss! Any place where it rains a great deal, ferns can take root on trees. If you ever visit a place where it rains a lot, such as Georgia or South Carolina, you can find many places where ferns and other plants are growing on trees.

Believe it or not, some plants have roots that are found both above the ground and underground. I am not talking about trees that have roots which peek out above the soil from time to

roots growing from the branches

The banyan tree has roots that grow from its branches in addition to the roots that grow underground.

time. I am talking about plants whose roots sometimes start growing underground and sometimes start growing *above ground!* Consider, for example, a banyan tree, which is pictured on the left. It has a root system that exists underground, but it also has roots that start in its branches and grow down towards the ground. Theses roots not only absorb water and nutrients from the soil, but they also help to support the long branches of the banyan tree. Because of this extra support, banyan tree branches can be very, very long. Consider, for example, a

banyan tree in Lahaina, Maui. It was planted in 1873 by a man named William Owen Smith, and its branches have grown so long that *this single tree covers a full square block in the city!*

Geotropism

God's design of roots is truly amazing. Think for a moment about what happens when you plant a seed. Do you have to worry about planting the seed "right side up?" No, you don't. No matter how you lay the seed into the dirt, the roots know to grow down into the soil. How do they know which way to grow? Well, God has given them a sense of which way is down. This sense is called **geotropism** (jee' oh trohp' is uhm). **Geo** refers to the **earth**, and **trop** means **turning**, so geotropism refers to the fact that the roots are always turning toward the earth.

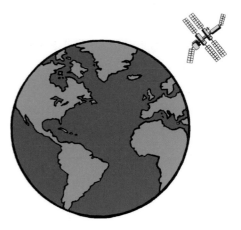

What causes geotropism? Well, plants have chemicals called **auxins** (awk' suns) that affect how they grow. Gravity causes different amounts of auxins at different places in the root. Because of this uneven distribution of auxins in the root, the root grows in the direction of gravity, which is towards the center of the earth.   When plants are grown in the Botany Science Lab in the International Space Station, roots do not always grow downward. They sometimes grow in the same direction as the stem! Since things in the International Space Station do not experience gravity, we can conclude that when a plant doesn't have gravity to guide it, its roots no longer know which way to grow. Because of this, geotropism is often called "gravotropism" (grav' oh trohp' is uhm), which means "turning in the direction of gravity."

What Do You Remember?

What are the three main purposes for roots? Explain why root hairs are important. What is the root cap? Where do roots add to their length? What are the roots always looking for? What is geotropism? What is another name for geotropism?

Root Systems

There are two main kinds of roots systems: **taproot systems** and **fibrous root systems**. A taproot system is made up of one thick main root growing down from the plant's stem. It has a number of smaller **secondary roots** branching off from this one main root, but a taproot system is deeper than it is wide. Often times, we eat taproots, such as carrots and turnips. Do you remember monocots and dicots from Lesson 2? Well, monocots typically do not have taproots. If a plant has a taproot, it is most likely a dicot.

A taproot system

A fibrous root system is made up of a series of roots growing in many directions. There may be a few roots that are thicker than others, but there is not one main root. A fibrous root system is usually wider than it is deep. Monocots typically have fibrous root systems, but not all fibrous root systems are from monocots. Some dicots also have fibrous root systems. As a result, the leaves and flowers are more accurate than the root systems when determining whether or not a plant is a monocot. Do you remember the distinguishing features of monocot leaves and flowers?

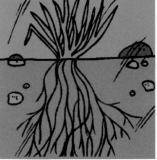

A fibrous root system

Geophytes

It is important to note that roots are not the only plant parts that you find underground. Onions, garlic, tulips, and many other plants grow from **bulbs**. Many people think that these bulbs are part of the root systems of the plants, but they are not. Roots grow out of the bottom of a bulb, but the bulb is actually a special underground storage house that is made up of special leaves and a short stem. A bulb operates kind of like a seed since you can pull it up and save it to plant later. Bulbs are called **geophytes** (jee' oh fites). **Geo** means **earth**, and **phyt** means **plant.** I guess they are called "earth plants" because they are like an entire plant under the earth. Bulbs are not the only geophytes. There are other underground storage systems in plants such as **corms**, **tubers**, and **rhizomes** (rye' zohms). Each can be kept in a cool place for years and then planted in the earth to grow! That is because each of these geophytes has all the nutrients the plant needs to grow its roots and stems! That sure does remind us of seeds, doesn't it?

Bulbs may look like they are a part of a plant's root system, but they are not.

A bulb looks a bit like a taproot, but each layer of a bulb is actually a special kind of leaf. Think about an onion. If you peel back the layers in an onion, you are actually peeling back leaves. A bulb is a source of constant renewal for a plant. In the winter, the above-ground portion of the plant dies, but the bulb continues to live below the surface. When spring comes, the bulb begins growing new stems and roots so that the plant grows back above the ground again.

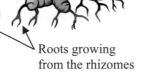

rhizomes

Roots growing from the rhizomes

Rhizomes look like roots, but they are actually underground stems that store excess food. Instead of growing down like roots do, they grow horizontally. If rhizomes are underground and look like roots, how do we know that they aren't roots? Remember, roots absorb water and nutrients for the rest of the plant. Rhizomes do not do this, so they are not roots. Roots *can* grow from rhizomes, as can leaves, flowers, and stems.

Corms are sometimes thought to be bulbs, but they are not. Bulbs have layers and layers of leaves, whereas corms are a solid food storage stem. They do not have layers that you can peel back. Corms grow roots from the bottom, however, just like bulbs, and they do survive underground during the winter, producing new plants in the spring. A crocus, often the first flower of spring, produces a corm.

A corm looks like a bulb but is not a bulb.

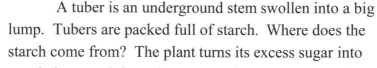

A tuber is an underground stem swollen into a big lump. Tubers are packed full of starch. Where does the starch come from? The plant turns its excess sugar into starch, because it is easier to store that way. Each tuber also has buds that can grow roots and stems. These buds are often called "eyes" on the most common tuber. This tuber is eaten every day by people all around the world. We call it a potato! As you can see, many geophytes are quite yummy!

Tubers are swollen stems full of starch.

Rooting

Most plants grow from seeds, and some plants can grow from geophytes. There is another way to grow a plant, however. It is called **rooting** a plant. To root a plant is to take a healthy stem or branch from the plant and put it in soil or water. Within a few weeks, something incredible happens! New roots begin to grow from the branch! With some plants you can even do this with just a leaf from the plant. Not all plants root easily. Some that do are: willow trees, African violets, ivy, geraniums, begonias, coleus, and roses. If you have any of these plants in your yard or neighborhood, try to root them in a vase of water. When you root a plant in water, you need to remove the bottom leaves from the stem and submerge the stem in the water. In a while, roots will emerge from the stem. Isn't that amazing? If you want to root a plant in soil rather than water, put a cut leaf, root, or stem in the soil and keep the soil moist. It can develop roots and grow into a whole new plant from that one cutting!

This stem from a lucky bamboo plant grew roots and leaves after it was put in water.

Interestingly enough, a plant grown by rooting is different from a plant grown from a seed. Plants grown by rooting are called **clones** of the plant from which the stem or root came. What is a clone? Well, a clone has all the same DNA as the plant from which the stem or root came. Do you know what DNA is? DNA is something that every living thing (including you) has! It contains all of the information that is needed for the living thing to grow and survive. For example, your DNA contains all of the information that your body needs to be able to eat, sleep, talk, or do anything else that you do. In other words, DNA is the "blueprint" that your body uses to become you! Every living thing has its own DNA, and that DNA contains the information needed for life. Well, a clone has the same exact DNA as the original. When a plant grows by rooting, then, its DNA is the same as the plant from which the root or stem was taken. In other words, it is a "copy" of the original plant. Please understand that this is not the case with a plant that grows from a seed.

Has someone told you that you have your father's eyes or perhaps your mother's hair? What did that person mean? He meant that your eyes look a lot like your father's eyes, or your hair looks a lot like your mother's hair. Most likely, you have some things in common with each of your parents. However, you don't look exactly like either of your parents, do you? That's because your DNA is a mixture of your mother's DNA and your father's DNA. This is what it's like for a plant that grows from a seed. The plant has a mixture of the DNA from the parent that produced the pollen and the DNA from the parent that received the pollen and made the seed. As a result, the new plant has things in common with its parent plants, but it is not a copy of either one of them. A plant that grows from a rooting, however, is really a copy of the original plant, because it has the same DNA as the original.

Tell someone about the two main types of root systems, and describe what each is. Also, explain all that you learned about geophytes and rooting.

Notebook Activities

Make an illustration for the roots lesson of your notebook. Write down (or dictate to your parent) what the roots do. In addition, make a drawing of what a root tip looks like under a microscope, using the picture on page 109 as a guide. Label the different parts of the root tip. Write down (or dictate to your parent) what geotropism is and what geophytes are.

Root Classification Hunt

Do you have weeds in your yard? If you do, today will be a fun day for you, because you are going on a root classification hunt! Begin by dressing in something that can get dirty, and put on some gloves. Garden gloves are best, but anything that will protect your hands will work. Go outside and begin pulling up weeds carefully, so as to preserve the roots. You may need to use a trowel or a metal spoon to dig around the roots so you can keep them intact, or whole, as you pull them up.

Younger Students: Sketch the different weeds you find and their root systems for your notebook. Note whether the root system is a taproot system or a fibrous root system.

Older Students: It's important to know what kind of weeds you have in your yard. You will want to include the weeds in your field guide book. Try to use a field guide such as a wild flower field guide to identify the weeds that you find. Make sketches of them and their root systems for your field guide. Also include any additional information you learn about them.

Project
Taproots

You will need:

- 2 carrots
- A knife
- 1 cup of water
- Blue food coloring

1. Have an adult use the knife to trim the pointed tip off both of the carrots.
2. Add 6 drops of food coloring to the cup of water and stir so that the water turns blue.
3. Place one carrot in the cup of blue water.
4. Place the cup with the carrot in your light hut or on a sunny window sill and wait 24 hours.
5. Keep the other carrot in the refrigerator.
6. What do you think will happen? Use a Scientific Speculation Sheet to record this experiment and what you believe the results will be. Do you expect anything to grow from these carrots? Do you believe the food coloring will show where water is absorbed into the carrot? How and where will see this? Do you think any secondary roots will begin to emerge?
7. After 24 hours, study both carrots. Are there any differences between the soaking carrot and the carrot in the refrigerator? If not, wait another 24 hours and check it again.
8. If you begin to see differences between the carrots, take the soaking carrot out of the colored water. What do you see happening to the carrot? Where is this happening?
9. Have an adult cut both carrots in half vertically making two long halves of each carrot from the top to the bottom.
10. Compare the carrots now that they have been cut in half. Explain what you think has happened to make the insides of the two carrots look the way they do.
11. Write all your thoughts, observations, and results on your Scientific Speculation Sheet and place it in your notebook.

Project
Force a Bulb

Did you know that you can trick a bulb into thinking it's spring during the middle of the winter? When we do that, we say we are **forcing the bulb**, because we are essentially forcing it to grow, even though it is winter. The indoor temperature of your house is about the same as a nice spring day. So, it would be fun to force a bulb in your house during the winter, because it is rare to see flowers bloom then.

You will need:

♦ A bulb from a plant (The best bulbs to force are paper white narcissus and hyacinths. Other bulbs will work, but do some research, because not all bulbs force easily.)
♦ A pot of soil (Remember, there should be drainage holes in the bottom.)
♦ Water
♦ A thermometer that reads in the 40° to 60° F range

1. Plant your bulb just below the surface of the soil in the pot.
2. Water the soil, and then set it in a dark, cool place. The temperature should be about 40° to 50° F for eight weeks. The meat drawer of your refrigerator is often in that temperature range, but you should use the thermometer to make sure.
3. Keep the soil evenly moist but not soggy.
4. When roots show at the hole in the bottom of the pot and top growth has begun, bring it into a cool spot about 50° to 60° F with subdued light for a week or two.
5. After a week or two, move the pot to a window (but not into direct sun) or under fluorescent lights. For best results, continue to keep it relatively cool (as if the bulbs were outside in the spring) as the buds develop and bloom.
6. The reason you needed to start by keeping the bulb in a cool place and then slowly moving it to slightly warmer places is to imitate the passing of winter. Bulbs are designed to stay dormant underground during the winter, so you need to "fool" the bulb into thinking that the winter has passed. However, some bulbs are pre-chilled. That means you do not have to keep them at cool temperatures when you are starting to grow them. You can begin growing a pre-chilled bulb the minute you get it home by planting it and placing it in a sunny window. You need not worry about imitating the passing of winter, because that has already been done by the company that sold you the pre-chilled bulb.

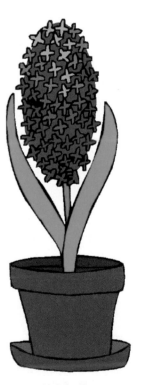

Hyacinth bulbs are fairly easy to force.

Lesson 8
Stems

Note to the teacher: Before you begin this lesson, take a stalk of celery that still has leaves on the end and place it in water that has been colored with blue or red food coloring.

What do you think gives you your shape? Could it be your skin? What about your muscles? These things help, but there is another important part of you that is responsible for a lot of your shape. Have another person stand up and bend over from the waist. Feel the ridge along his or her back. You have just felt that person's spinal column. The spinal column is the set of bones in our bodies that helps us stand up straight and tall. Our bones are a major part of what gives us our form. What would happen to you if all of your bones were removed? Why, you would fall into a heap upon the floor. Can you imagine that? How would you move about? Perhaps you would creep along the floor like a slug or a snail.

Without its stem, this foxglove plant could not hold up its leaves or flowers.

Well, believe it or not, plants also need to move. They don't need to move as much as you and I do, but they do need to move. They also need structures that give them form. Most of a plant's movement and structure come from its stems. Without stems, for example, plants would not be able to lift their lovely bodies above the ground. The stem is sort of like the spinal column of the plant, giving it its form.

Grass has leaves and stems, like most plants.

There are many different kinds of stems, so there are many different plant shapes and forms. Can you describe a tree stem? Tree stems are hard and woody, aren't they? What about the stem of the foxglove plant pictured above. Is it hard and woody? No, it is not. It is soft and green. You might be surprised to learn that even grass has stems. Because people mow their lawns, it is hard to get a good idea of what full-grown grass looks like. However, if you look at the photograph that is shown on the left, you will see that the grass in the picture has a stem. Grass also has stems that grow sideways along the ground. These stems are called **runners**. Many plants produce runners. If you ever visit a farm that grows strawberries, look at the strawberry plants. They have stems that grow upward, and they also have runners that grow along the ground.

Some plants have woody stems, while others have hollow stems. Some stems are as short as a clover stalk, and some are as long as a vine. Although there is a lot of variety in plant stems, one thing is for sure: all vascular plants have stems of one kind or another. Do you remember what a vascular plant is? It is a plant that has tubes which carry fluid throughout the plant. What runs through those tubes? That's right! Water! There is something else that runs through those tubes. Do you remember what that is? It is the sugary food that the leaves make for the plant. Water runs up from the roots to the leaves, and the sugary food comes down from the leaves to the rest of the plant.

Do you remember what the sugar-making, process is called? It is called photosynthesis. What color tells you that a plant is making sugar through photosynthesis? Remember, leaves are green because they have chlorophyll, which is necessary for photosynthesis. What color is the stem of a plant? Well, some stems are brown and woody, like a tree stem, but some stems are green. The stems of monocot plants are often green. What do you think that means? It means that the stems of these moncots actually do photosynthesis! Green stems, then, not only support a plant and give the plant form, but they also help to feed the plant as well.

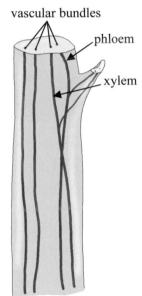

Though the outside of a green stem might be making sugar, the inside of the stem is full of water- and sugar-carrying tubes! After the leaf and the stem have made the sugary food, it is then sent back down into the plant to be used and stored.   Just like you have arteries and veins in your body that do different jobs, there are two different kinds of tubes inside vascular plants, and they do different jobs as well. The tubes that send the water up from the roots to the rest of the plant are called **xylem** (zy' lum). The tubes that send the sugary food down from the leaves to the rest of the plant are called **phloem** (floh' ehm). You can remember which is which because "phloem" sounds like "flow," which is what happens to the sugary food when it flows down to be used by the rest of the plant. Inside every stem are bundles of these xylem and phloem. These bundles are called **vascular bundles**.

The stem of a vascular plant contains vascular bundles of xylem and phloem.

Can you explain in your own words the difference between xylem and phloem?

Woody and Herbaceous Stems

Although all stems have vascular bundles, there are differences between stems as well. In fact, biologists typically classify a plant as either **woody** or **herbaceous** (her bay' shus) based on its stems. If a plant has stems that are hard and woody, it is not surprisingly called a woody plant. If the plant's stems are green and easy to bend, it is called an herbaceous plant. Well, it turns out that the stems of herbaceous plants and woody plants are quite different.

Of course, I have already told you one difference between woody and herbaceous stems. The soft, green stems of herbaceous plants perform photosynthesis, while woody stems do not. Another important difference between these two types of stems is how they grow. In general, herbaceous stems do not grow thicker with time. They grow longer by adding cells to the end of the stem. However, they do not grow thicker. Woody stems, however, grow thicker and thicker as the plant gets older and older.

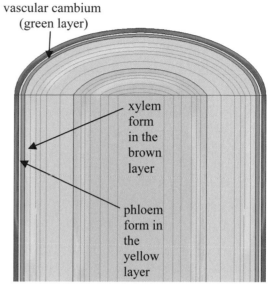

vascular cambium
(green layer)

xylem form in the brown layer

phloem form in the yellow layer

Woody stems grow thicker with age because they have something that herbaceous stems do not have. They have cells that make up a **vascular cambium** (cam' bee uhm). These cells are in a layer just inside the surface of the stem, as shown in the drawing to the right. They form xylem on one side of the layer and phloem on the other. This thickens the stem. As time goes on, the thickness of the stem continues to increase as the vascular cambium continues to make more xylem and more phloem. In other words, the cambium continues to add more and more wood to the stem, making it thicker and thicker.

There is something very interesting about the way woody stems grow in thickness. You see, the vascular cambium makes a lot of new wood during the spring and summer. As fall comes, it still makes new wood, but not nearly as much. In addition, the wood that it makes during the fall looks different from the wood it makes in the spring and summer. When winter comes, the vascular cambium stops making new wood, waiting until spring to begin again. Once spring comes, it starts making lots of new wood, and that new wood looks different from the wood that was made during the fall.

Each ring in this tree trunk represents one year of outward growth. If you count the number of rings, you can determine how old the tree was when it was cut down.

What does all of this mean? Well, look at the top of the drawing above. Do you see the rings that are in the wood? The thick parts of the rings are made up of the wood that was formed in the spring and summer, and the edges of the rings are made up of the wood that was formed in the fall. So each year, the stem forms a ring of wood which you can actually see if you look at the inside of the stem! Look at the picture on the left. It is a picture of a tree trunk, which is the biggest stem on a tree. What do you see? You see a bunch of rings. Each ring represents one year of growth.

Now think about what you just learned. Because of the way a woody stem thickens, it forms a new ring of wood each year. Because the inside of the ring is different in color than the outside of the ring, you can actually tell one ring from another. Suppose you see a tree that has been cut down. If you look at the inside of its trunk, you should be able to see rings, just as you saw in the picture on the previous page. Well, suppose you count those rings. What would you know? You would know *how many years the tree had lived before it was cut down!* Yes indeed, God has given us a way to tell how old a tree is! All we have to do is look at the inside of its trunk and count the rings. The next time you see a tree that has been cut down, try to count the rings on its trunk. That will tell you how many years the tree lived before it was cut down!

Now remember, the kind of growth I have been telling you about is how woody stems get *thicker*. Stems get longer in an entirely different way. Just like roots, stems grow longer by adding cells at their ends. Thus, the stem builds on top of itself in order to grow longer. Suppose you hammered a long nail into a tree two feet above the ground. In two hundred years, how high would that nail be? It would still be two feet above the ground. It might be deep inside the tree because the tree trunk got thicker every year, but it wouldn't move up as the tree grew, because the tree does not grow from the bottom.

The initials and paint on this tree will not rise as the tree grows.

Back in the olden days, people used to carve their initials into trees. Those initials would be in the same spot many years later when they came back to the tree, even though the tree had grown taller. This is because the tree grows taller by adding cells to its top and wider by adding rings. Eventually the initials might be covered up by the new bark that forms on the outside of the tree, but they will not rise as the tree grows, because a tree does not grow from the bottom. It grows from the top.

Cactus Stems

Some of the strangest stems that plants grow are those found on the cactus. You see, a cactus does not have leaves, because God designed it to live in dry places. Remember, leaves transpire, and that can waste water. The cactus conserves water by having no leaves. The green parts of the cactus are actually its stems! Since the stems are green, you know that they do the photosynthesis for the cactus. They also grow those prickly needles to protect the cactus from animals that want to eat it.

The cactus has no leaves. Its stems do all of the photosynthesis.

Auxins

Do you remember what a seed needs to grow? It only needs water, air, and warmth to germinate. But once it has used all the food within the cotyledon, the plant must produce food for itself. It does this through photosynthesis. Do you remember the four ingredients necessary for a plant to do photosynthesis? It needs chlorophyll, light, carbon dioxide, and water. In this part of the lesson, I want to concentrate on the fact that a plant needs light in order to do photosynthesis.

A plant needs light so much that the Lord created its stems with special chemicals called **auxins**. In the previous lesson, I told you about auxins and how they cause geotropism in plants. Now I want to tell you a little more about auxins and how they also cause **phototropism** (foh' toh trohp' iz uhm) in plants. Do you remember what geotropism means? It means "turning towards the earth." Well, you already know that "photo" refers to "light," so what do you think "phototropism" means? It means "turning towards the light."

It turns out that auxins make the stem of a plant bend and twist in order to grow towards the light. This is how the Lord designed all plants to reach towards the light as they grow. When something blocks light from a plant, auxins will cause the stem to bend, twist, and turn its way around the object to get to the sunshine. This is why we can sometimes see trees with strangely curved and circled branches when we go hiking. There have been trees that have bent into entire circles around other trees to get to the sunlight. In the photograph on the right, we see a very oddly-shaped tree trunk. It is likely that another tree fell on top of this tree at one time, but instead of dying, this tree's trunk grew around the tree that had fallen on it. The tree that fell eventually decayed away and crumbled into the ground below, leaving only this curved tree trunk as evidence of its fall.

The odd shape of this tree trunk can be explained by phototropism.

Scientists don't know all of the details of how auxins cause phototropism, but here's how they think it works: It seems that auxins are destroyed by light. As a result, there are very few auxins in the places where light is hitting a plant's stem. However, in places where very little or no light is hitting the stem, there are a lot of auxins. Well, botanists know that auxins cause the cells of stems to stretch out. This causes the stem to stretch wherever its cells stretch. This means that the parts of the stem which have little or no light hitting them will stretch, and the parts of the stem that have a lot of light hitting them will not stretch This causes the stem to turn in the direction of the light. Later, we will do an experiment with bean plants to see auxins in action. In the mean time, try this activity to understand the process.

Phototropism Activity

To see the way auxins cause stems to bend so that they can grow towards the light, perform the following activity.

You will need:
♦ Clay or Play-Doh®

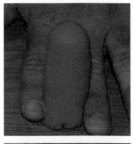

1. Roll the clay into a fat "snake" and stand the "snake" on a table. This "snake" will represent the stem of a plant.
2. Assume that one side of the stem is getting plenty of light but the other side of the stem is in darkness.
3. On whichever side you chose as the dark side, pinch the clay with your thumb and forefinger and pull *straight up* on the clay. This simulates what auxins do. They cause the stem to stretch on the dark side of the stem.
4. Notice what happens to the "stem" when you do that. It bends *towards* the side that you assumed was getting plenty of light. By causing the side of a stem that is in darkness to stretch, auxins bend the stem towards the light.

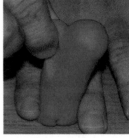

Examples of Phototropism

Although all plants have phototropism, there are some that really seem to *love* the light. As a result, they have extreme phototropism. Consider sunflowers, for example. They are extremely phototropic and can turn toward the light rather quickly. They literally turn their heads all day long to face the sun. Every sunflower in a field will face the sun all day long, because each flower twists its stems from the east to the west, following the sun as it travels across the sky. There is no mystery why they are called **sun**flowers, is there?

These sunflowers are all pointed in the same direction because they are all following the sun. As the sun moves in the sky, the sunflowers will all turn to follow it.

Daisies are another example of phototropism. The flower opens up with the sunlight and closes when the sun goes down. That is why it is called a "day's eye," or a daisy.

In the summer, you may notice that plants which are shaded are taller than the plants which grow in full sun. This is once again because of phototropism. The plants that are in the sun have plenty of light, so they tend to grow more outward than upward. Plants that are in the shade, however, are trying to find the light, so they tend to grow straight up. Remember the experiment you did in Lesson 2 with the bean seeds. The seed that germinated in the dark grew taller than the seed near the window. Next time you are observing plants in nature, look to see if some of them are taller than other plants of the same kind. If so, are they shaded under a tree or a bush that would make their stems grow longer? Notice also that plants which are big and bushy are usually in full sun.

Celery Experiment

Did you put celery in a cup of colored water at the beginning of this lesson? If not, you will want to grab some celery next time you go to the store so you can do this experiment.

Did you know that we eat the stems of the celery plant? That makes celery a vegetable. Do you remember the difference between a fruit and a vegetable? A fruit is a seed container. A vegetable is a part of the plant that has nothing to do with seeds. The big thick stems of the celery plant behave just like every other stem we have discussed in this lesson. Take your celery out of the colored water. Look at the bottom of the celery. Do you see the little dots on the bottom? Those are the xylem that pull water up to the leaves at the top of the celery plant. Since you used food coloring in the water, it is easy to see how the xylem pull water up to the leaves.

Put the celery back in the water and check on it tomorrow morning. See if there have been any significant changes to it. It is also a lot of fun to do this experiment with carnations.

Notebook Activities

Make an illustration for the stems portion of your notebook. Write down what you remember about xylem, phloem, and the vascular cambium. Explain how you can determine the age of a tree by looking at the inside of its trunk. Record what happened in the celery activity. Explain what auxins are and how they cause phototropism.

If you live near a thick forest or park, take a nature walk. Don't forget to bring along paper and colored pencils. Try to find branches that are twisted or turned in an odd shape. Try to determine how they grew to find the streaks of light coming through the forest tree tops. Draw them for your notebook and give an explanation for their odd shape.

Project
Seeking the Light

You will need:

♦ Two paper or Styrofoam® cups with lids (You should not be able to see light through them.)
♦ Two bean seeds
♦ Two peat pellets for germinating seeds
♦ A sharpened pencil
♦ Black paint or black permanent marker
♦ Black paper

1. Paint or color one cup with a marker to darken the cup.
2. If there is a hole in the lid, cover it with black paper. This will ensure that no light is able to penetrate this cup except through the hole that you are going to make in the next step.
3. Use the sharpened pencil to poke a small hole close to the bottom of the blackened cup. Make sure that the hole only allows a small amount of light into the cup. The hole needs to be close to the bottom so that it will be below the growing plant.

4. Do nothing to the second cup.
5. Soak the peat pellets in water.
6. Plant a bean seed inside each peat pellet.
7. Place a peat pellet inside each cup.
8. Use the lid you covered with black paper to cover the black cup. Do not cover the other cup.
9. Place the cups in your light hut or on a sunny window sill. Water your plants every three days. Do this only at night in a very dark room so that the plant in the dark cup does not get any light when you water it. Try not to disturb the plants too much when you water them.

10. What do you think will happen? Why do you think this? How long do you think it will take to for the results to be evident? Using a Scientific Speculation Sheet, record what you did, your hypothesis, and the results.

Lesson 9
Trees

Do you remember the story of Zacchaeus, who climbed a sycamore tree to get a glimpse of Jesus passing by (Luke 19:1-9)? Jesus stopped, knew his name, and told him he would be eating at Zacchaeus's house that day.

Have you ever climbed a tree like Zacchaeus? Trees are fun to climb, aren't they? When the weather is nice, perhaps you could go outside with a good book, climb to a thick branch of a tree, and find a nice cozy spot where you can sit back and read. There is nothing like the feeling of being in a tree.

Do you realize that the oldest living things on earth are trees? There are trees in California that were alive when Jesus was on the earth. In fact, they were alive long before then. In this lesson we will learn about these special trees.

This is one artist's idea of what the meeting between Zacchaeus and Jesus looked like.

The Role of Trees in Creation

This bald eagle built her nest in a tree to provide shelter for herself and her young.

God really gave mankind and the animals a special gift when He made trees. Trees provide the world with so much more than you might realize. They provide shelter, shade, beauty, food, and healthy air for humans and animals. Also, their roots help keep the entire structure of earth's landscape stable.

Look around your home and try to count all the things that come from trees. Do you have windows in your home? The frames around those windows are probably made of wood from trees. Do you have any wood on the outside of your home? Did you know that if you tore down all the walls in most houses, you would find that the entire frame of the house is made of wood? That means it comes from trees. What about your furniture? Is any of it made of wood? If so, it comes from trees. Even the book you are reading right now is made out of trees, because we make paper from trees! We are, indeed, very dependent upon trees. It was even a tree carved into a cross upon which Jesus hung to bear the sin of the entire world.

Trees are home to all sorts of animals: insects, birds, squirrels, lizards, frogs, etc. Without trees, these animals would have little protection from predators (other animals that want to eat them). The tree is their sanctuary, home, and in some cases, their food supply. Many animals and insects eat bark, leaves, twigs, and fruit. If you look underground where the tree roots are, you will find tunnels built by snakes, rabbits, moles, and many other kinds of burrowing animals. During the early days of life on earth, trees also provided food for the tallest land creatures, like apatosaurus, which was a dinosaur. Yes, even the dinosaurs, which many Christians think are mentioned in the books of Job and Psalms, feasted on the trees that God made.

This green crested lizard lives in the forest.

God designed the giraffe with a long neck so it could eat from trees.

Of course, since trees do a lot of photosynthesis, they also provide us with oxygen to breathe. Scientists have estimated that an acre of trees can make about 4,300 pounds of oxygen in one year. The average person needs about 730 pounds of oxygen per year. That means an acre of trees can provide about six people with all the oxygen they need! Of the many reasons God had for creating trees, we can see that having oxygen to breathe was an important one. Now it is important to realize that while plants (including trees) provide us with a lot of oxygen, they are not the only living things in creation that make this important chemical for us. In fact, more than half of the oxygen that we breathe is produced by microscopic creatures that live in the water and do photosynthesis there. So even though trees and other plants do give us oxygen, there are also other living things that give us oxygen.

Do you remember that plants help clean the air by removing pollutants? Well, trees do a lot of that work. A botanist with the U.S. Department of Agriculture Forest Service studied several major cities to see how much pollution the trees in those cities removed from the local air. What he found might surprise you. The trees in Denver, Colorado, for example, remove just over *a million pounds of pounds of pollutants each year*! That's just one city. The more trees a city has, the cleaner that city's air!

You learned in Lesson 7 that the roots of plants help hold the ground in place and reduce erosion. Well, trees do a lot of that work as well. Without the trees, much of the earth would be washed away into the oceans, lakes, and rivers during heavy rains and storms. The roots anchor the trees to the ground, but they also anchor the ground, reducing how much it is reshaped by wind and rain. Trees are a wonderful addition to God's creation aren't they?

Seed Making

Most trees are angiosperms. Do you remember what an angiosperm is? It is a plant that produces flowers. Many angiosperm trees produce what we call **imperfect flowers**. Do you remember what imperfect flowers are? We learned about them in Lesson 4. They have either male parts (stamens) or female parts (carpels), but unlike most flowers, they do not have both. Trees that produce imperfect flowers will produce flowers that have the male parts (carrying the pollen) and other flowers that have the female parts (carrying the eggs). The female flower will develop into a fruit (acorn, chestnut, etc.) once it has been pollinated.

Are there any trees that produce acorns in your neighborhood? If they produce acorns, they are oak trees. Did you know that an oak tree cannot reproduce until it is at least 20 years old? Some wait until they are 50 years old before they will produce their first acorns. Once an oak tree starts to produce acorns, it does so in a sporadic way. Unlike most angiosperms, which produce seeds regularly every season, an oak tree will have one year that it produces an enormous number of acorns. During such a year, the acorns simply cover the tree, and they fall from every limb. When this happens, they litter the ground with an overabundance of acorns. This is called **masting**.

Acorns grow on oak trees.

Squirrels try to find masting oak trees, because a single oak tree can produce as many as 2,000 acorns in one year! Since squirrels love acorns, they feast when they find a masting oak tree. For several years after that, however, the oak tree will only produce a few acorns, if any. Most oak trees

This squirrel is eating an acorn.

go through masting about once every five years. The chances of one acorn actually growing into an oak tree are very slim -- less than 1/10,000. That means that for every 10,000 acorns, only one will become a tree! This is because nine thousand nine hundred and ninety nine out of ten thousand will be eaten or used by animals in some other way. For example, an insect called the **acorn weevil** eats acorns, but it also deposits its egg inside them. The baby weevil, called a weevil larva, will grow up inside the acorn, eating its contents. If you find an acorn, it might have a little weevil larva living inside it. In fact, you may find an acorn shell that is completely hollow and has a tiny hole in it. That acorn was probably home to a weevil larva that ate the inside of the acorn and then burrowed out of it.

Tree Growth

Once an acorn (or any other seed) begins to grow into a plant, it is called a **seedling**. When a tree seed is developing into a tree, it is considered a seedling until it grows to be a few feet high. At that point, it is usually called a **sapling**. There may be some saplings growing in your neighborhood. If nothing harms them, they will one day grow to be mature trees.

A tree grows in three different ways. The roots grow longer each day in search of water and nutrients. The tree also grows taller, adding more cells to the tops of its branches as it reaches higher and higher. The tree also grows wider, producing a new ring of growth every year. Interestingly enough, botanists think that there is a limit to how tall any tree can grow. Because it gets harder and harder for a tree to get water to its topmost leaves as the tree grows taller, most botanists think that trees can never grow taller than about 420 feet. The tallest living tree is a redwood that is 369 feet high and is in the Humboldt Redwoods State Park in California. Even if trees have a limit to how high they can grow, there is no limit to their width. Since a tree adds a new ring of growth to its stems each year, the longer it lives, the wider its trunk and other stems become.

Redwood trees like these are the tallest trees in the world.

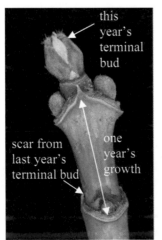

this year's terminal bud

scar from last year's terminal bud

one year's growth

You can actually see how much height a tree has added each year by studying one of its branches. There are marks along the twig of a tree branch that can tell us exactly how far a tree grew in each previous year. Farther down the twig, the branch becomes harder and more woody. This is where thick bark is beginning to form. At first, the bark is smooth and sleek, but with age, it thickens, and the surface dries and cracks. Twigs don't have thick bark like the trunk. This makes it easy to tell how much growth took place in a year.

At the tip of each twig, you will find a bud, which is called a **terminal bud**. In the spring, these buds sprout forth a group of petioles and leaves. The branch adds cells to the twig all summer, making it grow longer. Then, at the end of the growing season, a new terminal bud develops at the tip of the stem. On every twig, there is a circular scar where last winter's terminal bud was. By measuring the distance between the new terminal bud and the scar of last winter's terminal bud, you know how much the twig grew in one year.

Twig Anatomy

Every twig has several features. Learning those features will help you when you are studying twigs to examine their growth. As I already told you, the terminal bud is the bud at the very tip of the twig. In addition, a circular scar that surrounds the entire twig is called a terminal bud scar, and it represents where the terminal bud was the previous year. **Nodes** are places on a twig where other buds are located. Petioles, leaves, and eventually branches will grow from these buds. These buds are called **auxiliary** (awg zil' uh ree) **buds**, because they are not terminal buds, which must be at the tip of the twig. Below the auxiliary buds are leaf scars where leaves once were. The spaces between the nodes are called the **internodes.**

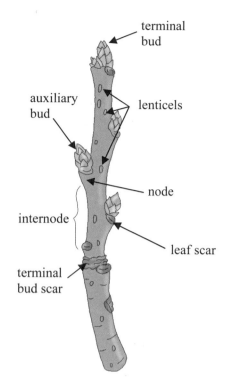

There are also small nicks scattered throughout each twig. They sometimes look like little blisters. These are actually little pores where the tree takes in oxygen! Although the leaves of a tree produce oxygen through photosynthesis, the cells of a tree need oxygen to survive, just like you and I do. These pores, called **lenticels** (len' tih selz), allow the twig to take in oxygen so that its cells can stay alive. I bet you didn't know a tree branch could breathe!

Notebook Activities
Twig Growth

The best time to do this activity is during the fall or winter. You can do this in the summer or spring, but the twig will be packed with leaves.

You will need:
- A ruler
- Colored pencils

1. Go outside and find a twig that is still on its tree.
2. Study the twig and try to find examples of all of the things pointed out in the drawing above.
3. Measure the distance between the terminal bud and the first terminal bud scar. That's the distance the tree grew during the previous spring and summer.
4. Moving down the twig, measure the distances between successive terminal bud scars. Which year did the twig grow the most? Which year did it grow the least?
5. Take the twig inside and make a drawing for your notebook. Be sure to label all of the structures that you identified in step #2.

Estimating the Height of a Tree

Have you ever wanted to know how tall a tree is? You might think that there is no way to measure the height of a tree, because you don't have a measuring tape long enough to measure such a thing. Even if you did, how would you climb to the top of the tree to use it? Well, you can get a very good idea of how tall a tree is with just a ruler and the help of a friend whose height you know.

You will need:
- Someone to help you
- A measuring tape or yardstick to measure the height of your helper
- A 12-inch ruler
- A tall tree

1. Use the tape measure to measure how tall your friend is.
2. Take your friend outside and find a tall tree.
3. Have your friend stand right next to the tree trunk.
4. Walk about 15 feet away from the tree.
5. Hold the 12-inch ruler at arm's length, between you and the tree. Hold it so that the tree looks like it's right next to the ruler.
6. Pull the ruler back towards your face until the ruler looks like it is as tall as the tree. If the ruler appears smaller than the tree no matter how close you get it to your face, walk farther away from the tree and try again. If the ruler is taller than the tree even when you are holding it out at arm's length, walk closer to the tree.
7. Once you have gotten the ruler to a point where it looks like it is as tall as the tree, hold it right at that position and turn your body (without moving your arm) so that your helper now looks like he is right next to the ruler.
8. Use the numbers on the ruler to measure how tall your helper appears to be.
9. Take the measurement from step #8 and divide it into 12. For example, if my helper appears to be 2 inches tall based on the ruler, I would divide 12 by 2 to get 6.
10. Take the answer you got in step #9 and multiply it by the actual height of your helper, which you measured in step #1. If my helper was 5 and ½ feet tall, for example, I would take my answer from step #9 (which was 6) and multiply it by 5 and ½ feet to get 33 feet. That is the height of the tree!

This activity makes use of a math concept called "proportionality." By holding the ruler close to your eye, you made the ruler appear as big as the tree. When you then used that same ruler at that same position to measure something with a known height (your helper), you were able to determine the height of the tree relative to the height of your helper. In the examples that I gave you, my helper appeared to be 2 inches tall using the ruler. Since the tree appeared to be the same height as the ruler, I knew that the tree was 6 times taller than my helper. Proportionally, then, the height of the tree was equal to 6 times the height of my helper.

What Do You Remember?

What are some reasons God made trees? How can you tell how much a tree has grown by its branch? Explain the anatomy of a twig. Be sure to include terminal buds, lenticels, nodes, internodes, and auxiliary buds in your explanation.

Growing Outward

A tree's trunk is its main stem. As the tree trunk and branches get thicker and thicker each year, they also have important work to do. The part of the tree right under its bark is where most of the tree's activity actually takes place. Right under the bark, you find the phloem, and right under the phloem you find the vascular cambium. Right under that, you find the xylem. Do you remember what xylem and phloem are? The xylem suck the water up from the roots and send it to the leaves, while the phloem cause the sugary food to flow down to be used and stored by the rest of the tree. Do you remember what the vascular cambium is? That's the layer of cells which makes the xylem and phloem, causing the tree's trunk to get wider each year. All this is happening right underneath the bark!

What is the bark? The bark is the shield of protection for the xylem, phloem, and vascular cambium. If you peel off the bark, you will likely peel off some of the phloem as well, robbing the tree of some of its most important cells! What do you think would happen if you pulled all the bark off a tree? In some ways, it would be like peeling off all of your skin! If someone peeled off your skin, you would lose water and nutrients, and you would certainly get diseases, because your skin protects the inside of your body. In the same way, a tree's bark is its protection! Some trees shed their bark and replace it with new bark. If a tree has loose bark, it might be getting ready to shed its bark.

This birch tree is shedding its bark. Notice the new bark underneath the old bark.

The Layers in a Tree Trunk

Look outside at a tree. Do you realize that although the tree is alive, the very core of the tree trunk is actually dead wood? Yes, indeed. The wood on the very inside of the tree is called the **heartwood**. It is wood that once was living, but is now quite dead. When the tree was young, what is now the heartwood *was* the xylem that sucked water up from the roots to the leaves. However, as layers of xylem and phloem were added each year, the old xylem got plugged up and actually died. When that happened, it became heartwood. Even though it no longer carries water for the tree, it still does an important job. The heartwood helps a tree to survive through strong winds by giving the tree strength. Sometimes, termites or wood ants can eat away at the heartwood, making the tree mostly hollow on the inside. Trees without heartwood can continue to grow for hundreds of years, however, because the outer layers are the living parts of the tree. Of course, such a tree can topple over more easily because it doesn't have thick heartwood in the center to support it.

A tree trunk can be separated into five different layers: the heartwood, the sapwood, the vascular cambium, the inner bark, and the outer bark. Each of these layers has a different job:

➢ The heartwood is the dead wood in the very center of the tree trunk. It gives the trunk strength.

➢ The **sapwood** surrounds the heartwood and is made of xylem that transport water up from roots to the leaves. It also stores the excess food that the leaves make during the summer in the form of starch. In the early spring, the tree starts converting that starch into sugar, and the sugar starts to run in the sapwood. In the sugar maple, the sugar that is flowing in the sapwood gives us maple syrup.

➢ The **vascular cambium** is a thin layer of cells that produces new xylem and phloem. It causes the tree trunk to get wider every year.

➢ The **inner bark** is made up of the phloem. It transports food from the leaves downward to the rest of the tree.

➢ The **bark** is the outer layer of the tree, and it provides protection for the living parts of the tree. The outer bark is often called the **cork** of the tree.

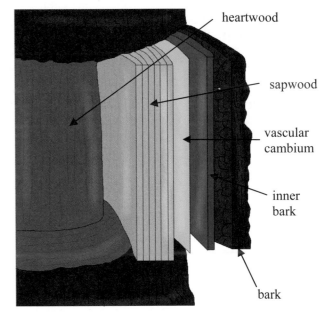

heartwood

sapwood

vascular cambium

inner bark

bark

Thirsty Trees

Trees transport enormous quantities of water from their roots to their leaves, and the water moves at speeds of up to 25 feet per hour. Some of that water is used for photosynthesis. Do you remember what happens with the excess water? It transpires. That means it moves out of the leaf and into the air. Do you realize that a tree uses less than two percent of the water taken in from the roots for photosynthesis? More than 90% if the water is transpired! A tree can transpire enormous amounts of water into the atmosphere from its leaves every day. Tons of water taken from the soil by the roots is released into the air each day by trees. Yes, I said tons! That is more than a car weighs! Not all trees transpire so much, however. Some trees, called conifers, don't transpire much at all. You will learn about those trees in the next lesson.

Tree Identification

This world has thousands of varieties of trees, but there are really only two basic kinds of trees: angiosperms and gymnosperms. Gymnosperm trees make their seeds in open vessels like pinecones, and angiosperm trees make their seeds in closed vessels that we call fruits. Gymnosperm trees usually have needles (like pine trees) or scaled leaves (like juniper trees), while angiosperm trees have broad or flat leaves (like oak trees).

There are many different trees in this photo, including both gymnosperms and angiosperms.

It will be fun to identify all the trees in your yard or neighborhood with a field guide. A field guide will usually divide the trees into groups by the shapes of their leaves. In the project at the end of this lesson, you will make a sketch of each tree in your area, taking note of its shape and size. You will also want to note the shape, margin, venation, and texture of its leaves, and you will want to describe its fruit. Finally, you will note whether it is deciduous (loses its leaves in the winter) or evergreen (stays green throughout the winter).

When noticing the shape of the tree, look at the shape of the trunk as well as the **crown** (top) of the tree. Is the crown shaped like an "A," a circle, or another shape? Most field guides will show an outline or silhouette of the tree. This helps you to identify what kind of tree it is. Look carefully at the trees in your area and draw what you observe.

Another important way to identify trees is by the texture, shape, and feel of their bark. During the spring and summer, it is easiest to identify trees by their leaves and fruit. During the winter, however, it is very difficult to do this. Because of this, there are some good field guides that show you how to identify a tree by its bark.

If you study the bark on trees, you will notice that every tree has its own bark pattern. Beech trees have smooth, flaky bark, while oak trees develop deep, long ridges in their bark. Shagbark hickory trees have shaggy bark (of course!), while the ash has gray bark with a diamond shape pattern running down it. Birch trees have paper-thin bark (once used by Native Americans to make canoes), while the bark of the sequoia trees in California might be more than a foot thick with deep ridges! The bark of young trees is smoother than that of old trees. As the tree grows, its bark either gets thicker and thicker, or on some trees, it sheds off as new bark replaces it.

Tell someone what you have learned about heartwood, sapwood, vascular cambium, inner bark, and outer bark. Also, explain to this person why a tree with no heartwood can still live.

Notebook Activities

Draw an illustration of the five different layers in a tree's trunk. You can use the drawing on page 132 as a guide. Be sure to label each layer and describe what it does for the tree.

Bark Rubbings

In this activity, you are going to make bark rubbings for your notebook. As I told you earlier, each tree has its own special pattern of bark, and you will be able to make a copy of this pattern by doing a bark rubbing. This will help you to identify the tree. If you are making a field guide, you should include a bark rubbing for each tree that you are putting in your field guide.

You will need:
- ♦ A crayon with all the paper removed
- ♦ Plain white paper
- ♦ Tacks (optional)

1. Lay the paper across a tree trunk.
2. If you have tacks, use them to secure the paper to the tree. You do not need to do this, because you can just hold the paper with your hands, but tacks might make the job easier.
3. Holding the crayon sideways, rub it over the paper. As you do this, you will see that the crayon makes marks on the paper in the pattern of the tree's bark. This is a bark rubbing.
4. Put the bark rubbing in your notebook, including the kind of tree from which it came.

Project
Identifying Trees

For this project, I want you to identify the trees you have in your yard or neighborhood using a field guide. If it is spring or summer, you can use leaves and fruits to identify the tree, which is the way most field guides do it. If you are in a cold region or it is the middle of winter, you will want a field guide that identifies trees by their bark patterns, such as: *Tree Bark: A Color Guide, Trees: Trees Identified by Leaf, Bark & Seed* (part of the Fandex Family Field Guides series), or *A Field Guide to Trees and Shrubs* (part of the Peterson Field Guide series).

Lesson 10
Gymnosperms

Since Lesson 3, we have been concentrating on the angiosperms, which are the plants that make their seeds from pollinated flowers. We have discussed some things that are common to all vascular plants, but mostly, we have talked about angiosperms. Well, now it's time to move on and talk about the other type of seed-making plants in creation: the gymnosperms.

When you walk outside, do you ever find pinecones on the ground? Those are the seed containers for a very popular group of gymnosperms: the **conifers**. If you remember way back to

Lesson 1, you might recall that gymnosperms produce uncovered seeds. Well, the most common gymnosperms are called conifers, and they produce seeds that are nestled on the slats of an open cone. Since the cones are open to the air, the seeds are uncovered, and that's why conifers are gymnosperms. In fact, "conifer" means "cone-bearer." Conifers are very special and have very different features from the flowering plants we have studied.

In cooler areas, almost all the trees you find are conifers. In fact, if you look at a globe, cone-making plants are the main trees you find from Canada, across to Siberia, and all the way to Norway. They practically circle the top of the globe. Conifers are very special because they are the largest and oldest trees

This giant sequoia tree is a conifer because it produces its seeds in cones.

found on earth. They seem able to survive the longest of any other tree. In fact, some conifers living today were seedlings when the earliest civilizations began emerging after the Flood. Many of the giant sequoias in the Pacific Northwest of the U.S. are more than 3,000 years old!

Not only are giant sequoia trees old, they are simply gigantic! Some reach more than 300 feet into the sky. It is difficult to photograph the whole tree. It goes up hundreds of feet into the air. Just the bark alone can be two feet thick! When the early settlers cut these mammoth trees down, they used the tree stump as a dance floor for the whole town. The wood of one tree was enough to build several houses and barns for the town.

This giant sequoia has fallen down. Notice the lady sitting on the tree and how tiny she appears compared to the tree.

The giant sequoia is probably the most famous tree in the world. When the settlers first arrived in Oregon and California, no one except the Native Americans of that area knew that trees could grow as big as they do. These trees were giants when Jesus walked upon the earth. Giant sequoias are the largest members of a group of trees called "redwood trees." They get their name from the fact that they are somewhat red in color. In fact, the first Spanish explorer to see redwoods called them "palo colorado," which meant "red tree."

Creation Confirmation

Although the giant sequoias are the biggest trees on earth, they are not the oldest. The oldest trees on earth are also found in the United States of America. They are called **bristlecone pines** and, like the giant sequoias, they are found in California. There is one bristlecone pine named "Methuselah" that is the oldest living tree on this earth. Scientists bored a small hole through the tree's trunk so that they could count its rings, and they found that it is just over 4,700 years old!

Trees like these bristlecone pines are the oldest on the earth.

Methuselah was the name of Noah's grandfather, and he lived the longest of anyone in the Bible. I'm sure Noah learned a lot from Methuselah, and we can learn a lot from the bristlecone pine tree called Methuselah. You see, this old pine tree gives us a reason to believe the Bible.

Think about it. The oldest living tree is just over 4,700 years old. How long ago does the Bible say the worldwide Flood happened? It doesn't give an exact date, but people who study the Bible and its history say that the Flood occurred about 4,700 years ago. They estimate this age by counting the generations of people that have been recorded in the Bible since the time of Noah.

Some people say there was no worldwide Flood. If that is true, however, why are there no trees that are older than 4,700 years? Botanists know that bristlecone pine trees can live for thousands more years than the oldest recorded age of 4,700 years. So, why are there none that are older than that? There are no trees older than that because the worldwide Flood occurred about 4,700 years ago. No trees would have survived the Flood, but their seeds did. Thus, no tree can be older than the Flood. If there were no worldwide Flood, we would find numerous bristlecone pines much older than 4,700 years old. There are no such trees; however, which tells us that the worldwide Flood did occur, just as the Bible says.

What Do You Remember?

Where are the largest trees in the world found? What kind of trees are they? Where are the oldest trees in the world found? What kind of trees are they? What is the name of the oldest tree in the world? How does it provide evidence for the account of the worldwide Flood reported in the Bible?

Softwood

Gymnosperm trees are often called **softwood** trees, while angiosperm trees are generally called **hardwood** trees. Why do you think they might be called by these names? Which kind of tree do you think would be easier to cut down? Softwood trees are usually a lot easier to chop down than hardwoods. In fact, thousands are chopped down every year and used as Christmas trees all over the world! Even a child could chop down a small Christmas tree. This is because the wood of gymnosperm trees is generally much softer and easier to cut. Most furniture is made from pine because of this. It's easier to work with when you are cutting and sanding it to make furniture. It is also easier to lift, carry, and move around. Oak, cherry and maple furniture is made from angiosperm trees. That kind of furniture is heavier, and it is harder to make. Which kind of wooden furniture do you have in your home? Compare how difficult it is to lift one chair with another made from a different wood. Try to guess which wood is pine and which is oak, maple, or cherry. Sometimes the manufacturer will stamp the type of wood on the bottom of the furniture. Does your furniture have such a stamp?

Evergreen

Most conifers keep their leaves even through the winter. When a tree is green all winter long, it is called an **evergreen** tree. These trees are different from deciduous trees, which lose their leaves in the fall. Which is the most plentiful tree in your area: deciduous or evergreen? Most angiosperm trees are deciduous, while most conifers are evergreen. One notable exception is the larch. It is a conifer, but it is deciduous.

Do you remember why deciduous trees have to lose their leaves in the autumn? It's because of transpiration. Deciduous trees lose so much water through their big leaves that they would die of thirst in the frozen, dry winter. Evergreen leaves, which are usually needle-like, awl-like, or scale-like, are designed so that they hold water inside of themselves. As a result, they don't transpire very much, so the tree doesn't need to lose its leaves by winter.

Most conifers stay green, even throughout the winter.

Now please understand that evergreens actually *do* lose their leaves, just not all at once. All throughout the year, they will lose some leaves, but then new leaves will grow back to replace them. These trees dominate the cold regions of the earth because deciduous trees can't survive as well there. High up on a snowy mountain, where the snow is present for many months of the year, it is hard for deciduous trees to conserve water. Conifers, on the other hand, do not lose much water through transpiration. As a result, they are perfectly suited to winter climates. Believe it or not, conifers also grow well in warm, dry regions because of their uncanny ability to hold on to every bit of water they can get.

The dead pine needles on the ground in this picture show that even evergreen trees lose their leaves.

Notebook Activity
Comparing Transpiration

If you have a conifer and a deciduous tree with leaves that are still green in your yard, you can do an experiment to measure how much water each transpires in a week. Do you remember when you put a plastic bag over the leaf of a houseplant to see transpiration in action? You are going to do a similar thing, but this time you will do it on outdoor trees.

You will need:
- Two plastic sandwich bags
- Two clothespins

1. Put one sandwich bag around a large leaf of a deciduous tree outside.
2. Secure the sandwich bag with a clothespin.
3. Put the other sandwich bag around a little clump of leaves of a conifer outside.
4. Every few days, go outside and check the amount of water in each of the bags. You can leave them on the trees all summer long if you like.
5. Use a Scientific Speculation Sheet to write down which bag you think will have more water in it. Record whether or not your hypothesis was correct.

Explain to someone why an evergreen tree is well suited for both cold, wintery climates as well as hot, dry climates. Also, explain why gymnosperm trees are often called softwood trees.

Gymnosperm Leaves

There are three kinds of leaves found on conifers: **needle-like**, **scale-like**, and **awl-like**. Needles are smooth and straight. Sometimes they are long, and sometimes they are short. They are usually pointy at the tip. Scale-like leaves have a bumpy texture that looks like scales. They appear almost like snake skin. They are rough, and often have a strong scent that reminds us of Christmas. Awl-like leaves are not scaled, nor are they long, pointy needles. They are pointy leaves that look a little like very thin triangles or flat spikes.

| needle-like leaves | scale-like leaves | awl-like leaves |

What kinds of leaves are on the conifers in your area? Draw pictures of each leaf type for your notebook. On your next nature walk, try to find conifers with each kind of leaf structure.

In addition to having different leaves from angiosperm trees, conifers are usually shaped differently than angiosperm trees. Often, they are shaped like a skinny "A." This shape allows a lot of snow to fall off the tree rather than stay trapped in the leaves. That way, the limbs are less likely to break during heavy snows in the winter. The soft wood of the tree also allows its limbs to bend down when weighted with snow so that the snow can slide off the tree. If a hardwood tree branch is weighted down with snow, the branch may get so heavy that it simply snaps off. You can see how God designed conifers in a very special and practical way!

The shape and soft wood of a conifer help it to deal with snow.

Cones

Now remember, conifers are not the only kind of gymnosperms that exist. However, they are the most common gymnosperms, so that's why we are concentrating on them. Do you remember what separates conifers from other gymnosperms? Conifers make their seeds in cones. Have you ever seen a pinecone? Most people have. In fact, you have probably held a pinecone in your hand at one time or another. You might even have a pinecone sitting outside in your yard right at this moment. We'll be doing an experiment with pinecones at the end of this lesson, so you will want to collect one soon. Well, a pinecone is an example of a cone made by a conifer.

Each conifer makes two different types of cones: **pollen cones** (which contain pollen) and **seed cones** (which contain eggs). Can you guess which one is the male cone and which one is the female cone? From our study of flowers, you probably guessed that the pollen cones are the males and the seed cones are the females. Both male and female cones usually grow on the same tree. The female cones are by far the most noticeable. They are usually reddish-brown or greenish-yellow when they first begin to grow, but after they are pollinated, they will turn into the dark, woody-looking cone you have seen on the ground.

Pollen cones are generally softer and harder to see than seed cones. In fact, you might not have noticed them before. Without the pollen cones, however, the seed cones would never develop new seeds. After all, in order for a seed to form, an egg must be pollinated. Angiosperms use flowers to make sure that the eggs get pollinated, while conifers use cones. The pollen cones produce pollen in the spring. When it is ready, the pollen cone bursts open, and millions of pollen grains fly into the air, some landing on the ground, some landing in nearby water, and some reaching their target: a seed cone. After its pollen is released, the pollen cone is no longer needed, so it shrivels up and dies.

Pollen cones are softer and less noticeable than seed cones.

The seed cones are usually what we notice on a conifer.

The female cone has scales that look something like leaves. At the base of each scale, there are two ovules, which contain the eggs. Once the pollen reaches the eggs, it takes more than a year for the eggs to be completely fertilized, and the egg must be fertilized in order for the seed to form. When the year is over and the eggs are fertilized, the seeds begin to mature.

When the seeds are ready, the pinecone is also ready. On a warm, dry day, the pinecone expands, opening its scales so that the seeds can fall out. Each seed is attached to a little wing (often called a **key**), which will help it float to a new plot of land to grow into a new tree. If the day is cold and wet, the pinecone is designed to stay shut, holding onto its seeds until a warm, dry wind blows in.

Forest Fires

Forest fires can destroy thousands of trees in a very short amount of time. In 1988, for example, a series of forest fires swept through a large portion of Yellowstone National Park. Nine of those fires were started by careless human beings, but 42 of them were started naturally, by lightning striking dry wood. More than 790,000 acres, which is about 35% of the park, were affected by these fires.

Although forest fires can cause a lot of damage, they can also be beneficial to a forest. In a typical fire, some large trees (especially the ones with a lot of moisture in their sapwood) will survive. The other trees will burn away, but that can actually be a good thing. The decayed remains of burned trees fertilize the soil, and the cleared landscape can become home to a larger variety of plant species than was there before. In fact, based on many observations that scientists have made over many years, it has been determined that trying to suppress natural forest fires actually *reduces* the variety of plant and animal species that are seen in the wilderness. As a result, those who care for our national forests tend to let forest fires burn without restriction, as long as they pose no threat to people, homes, or buildings.

Berry-like Cones

As you study God's incredible creation, you will find that it often does not obey the "rules" that human science tries to impose on it. Juniper bushes and trees provide a good example of this. Botanists called junipers conifers, and even though "conifer" means "cone-bearer," junipers do not bear cones. Why are they called conifers? Well, juniper leaves and wood are so similar to conifer leaves and wood that it only makes sense to group them with the conifers, despite the fact that they don't make cones. To make this even more confusing, botanists insist on calling juniper fruits "cones," even though they clearly look like berries.

Despite the fact that junipers bear flowers and produce fruit, they are considered conifers. Their fruits are even called cones.

A given juniper will produce only pollen or only eggs. Because of this, only the "female" junipers (the ones with eggs) will bear fruit, because fruit must come from an egg that has been pollinated.

Juniper leaves can be scale-like or awl-like, but one thing is the same with all junipers: they have a strong odor that you can smell from a long way off. Junipers are often bushes and shrubs, though there are many kinds of juniper trees as well.

The yew is another conifer that doesn't make cones. It makes an **aril** (ar' uhl), which is a fleshy covering for the seed that looks a lot like a fruit. It is sometimes called a "false fruit." The arils of a yew are quite poisonous to eat, but yews have a natural chemical in them called "taxol," which has been demonstrated to be effective in the treatment of certain types of cancer.

What Do You Remember?

What are the three kinds of leaves that conifers can have? What is the process by which conifers produce seeds? How long does it take for an egg to be fertilized? How can forest fires be beneficial to a forest? Name two conifers that don't produce cones.

Two Other Interesting Gymnosperms

Even though I have been concentrating on conifers as typical gymnosperms, there are gymnosperms that are not conifers. These gymnosperms are put in different phyla from the conifer phylum. One such gymnosperm is the **cycad** (sy' kad). Cycads grow in warm areas, where palm trees are found, and they are often mistaken for palm trees, because cycads and palms both have a trunk topped by a whorl of palm-like leaves, usually without any side branches. The leaves of cycads, like palms, have a central stalk with rows of narrow leaflets on both sides. The similarities between these two plants end, however, when it is time to make seeds.

Despite the fact that you might think this is a palm, this is actually a cycad.

Palms bear flowers which, when fertilized, make fruits such as dates and coconuts; therefore, palms are angiosperms. Cycads, on the other hand, produce cones in the center of the leaf whorl, with male and female cones occurring on separate plants. Because their seeds are made in open containers rather than closed fruits, cycads are gymnosperms. The funny thing about cycads is that even though they do make cones, like conifers, they are not called conifers because their leaves and wood are very different from conifer leaves and wood. The next time you think you see a palm tree, look twice. It might not be what you think. See if there is any fruit on the tree. If there is fruit on the tree, it is a palm tree. If there are cones on the tree, it is a cycad.

Ginkgo Biloba

The **ginkgo** (geenk' oh) is a most unusual little gymnosperm, for its leaves are broad and flat like those of an angiosperm. It also loses its leaves in the fall and regrows them in the spring, which means it is deciduous. Despite the fact that ginkgo leaves are similar to angiosperm leaves, it is a gymnosperm because it produces uncovered seeds.

Ginkgo leaves look like angiosperm leaves, even though the ginkgo is a gymnosperm.

Like the junipers, ginkgos produce either pollen or eggs. Thus, there are "male" ginkgo plants and "female" ginkgo plants. A female ginkgo, like the oak tree, must be at least 20 years old before it can make seeds, which are about one inch round and a yellowish color. When the seed coat comes off, the fleshy interior creates a terrible odor, smelling like vomit. Because of this, people don't plant female trees for ornamental purposes. This makes the male tree much more valuable to people than the female tree. Before the late 1600s, scientists had found fossils of ginkgo tree leaves but had never found any ginkgo trees that were alive. Because of this, the ginkgo was thought to be a plant that once lived on earth but no longer does. When a type of living thing is no longer found living on earth, we say that it went **extinct** sometime during earth's past. It was thought that the ginkgo was extinct, until a single species, *Ginkgo biloba*, was discovered in 1691 in Japan. Japanese herbalists had been using ginkgo seeds as medicine for hundreds of years.

What Do You Remember?

Why are cycads considered gymnosperms? Describe a cycad. Describe the ginkgo. Why are ginkgos considered gymnosperms? What are some differences between them and other gymnosperms? Why do people prefer to plant the male *Ginkgo biloba*?

Notebook Activities

Younger Students: After you have recorded all you remember from this lesson, draw a picture of you standing next to a giant sequoia. Try to make the height of the tree realistic compared to your height.

Older Students: Record and illustrate all that you learned. Be certain to include why gymnosperms are able to survive cold climates and how cones are formed.

Persuasive Speech

Write out a speech explaining why bristlecone pine trees give evidence for the Bible's account of the worldwide Flood. After your speech is written, practice it over and over again until you have it memorized. At that point, write down a few key words to put on a notecard. Those words should be designed to help "jog your memory" as you give the speech. Give your speech in front of a group of people.

A Tree Grows Up

I want you to write a story of the life of a bristlecone pine. I want your story to have a parallel story of what was going on in history during the beginning of its life. For example, you might begin the story by saying: "When the pinecone seed rested upon dry ground, it began to grow. At this time, Noah was leaving the ark with his family." You could then write about what happened to the tree and what happened to Noah and his family at the same time.

Project
Opening and Closing Pinecones

Pinecones are programmed by God to open and close according to the outside temperature and humidity. What do you think would happen if you put a pinecone in a bucket of cold water? What do you think would happen if you placed the pinecone in a heated oven? Record what you think will happen on a Scientific Speculation Sheet.

You will need:
- Pinecone
- Oven preheated to 250 degrees
- Bucket of cold water

1. Place the pinecone in the bucket of cold water.
2. Check your pinecone in an hour. Has it made any changes? Record what you observed on the Scientific Speculation Sheet.
3. Place the pinecone in an oven that has been preheated to 250 degrees. Check your pinecone in an hour. Has it made any changes? Record what you observed on the Scientific Speculation Sheet.
4. If you find a seed deep inside your pinecone, why not plant it and grow a tree inside your light hut?

Lesson 11
Seedless Vascular Plants

There are only a few kinds of vascular plants that don't produce seeds. Instead, they produce **sporangia**. Do you remember what sporangia are? You learned about them in Lesson 1. **Angia** means **container**; so **sporangia** means **spore container**. These plants make spore containers, each of which holds many spores. These spores can grow into new plants, but they are *not* seeds.

Do you remember what a seed is? A seed is a plant embryo in a protective coat that contains food for the embryo so that it can germinate. In other words, it is a baby plant in a box with its lunch. Spores are not like that at all. Individual spores are very tiny, and they have no food inside of them. Do you realize what that means? In order for a seed to germinate, it does not need soil or light right away, because it uses the food stored in the seed to start growing. A spore does not have any food, so if it is to germinate, it must have soil (or a suitable substitute) and light right away, because it must start making its own food right away.

In this lesson we will study the vascular plants that produce sporangia rather than seeds. Now remember what "vascular" means. It means that the plants have tubes that carry fluid inside them. So the plants that we will study in this lesson have tubes inside them, but they do not produce seeds. You have seen such plants before. The most abundant type of seedless vascular plant is the fern.

There are several things that make ferns different from other vascular plants. One is that they are very delicate and only flourish in very moist conditions. Ferns do not like hot, dry areas like flowering plants and conifers. They like to be out of direct sunlight, sheltered under the canopy of a forest or trees. A forest canopy is something like a tent over the forest formed by the leaves of the tall trees in the forest. Do you think there might be a lot of ferns growing under the sequoia trees in California? Indeed, the thick canopy provided by the tall sequoia trees is just ideal for the growth of ferns.

The ferns growing from this forest floor are seedless vascular plants.

Fronds

The leafy branch of a fern is called a frond. Do you remember what compound leaves are? You learned about them in Lesson 6. A compound leaf is a leaf made up of many individual leaflets. Well, the fronds of some ferns are actually doubly-compound. You see, a frond is composed of a central stalk called a **rachis** (ray' kus). It is an extension of the petiole, which connects the frond to the stem of the fern. The leaflets that attach to the rachis are called **pinnae** (pin' ee), and those pinnae are often made up of more individual leaflets, as is the case in the frond pictured to the right. That's why I say that some fronds are doubly-compound leaves. They are compound because the pinnae are individual leaflets attached to the central rachis, but then those pinnae are often compound leaves, being made up of many small leaflets.

This frond is one fern leaf.

If you look on the underside of a frond, you will often find little growths stuck there. These little growths are clusters of sporangia, and those sporangia contain the spores that will grow into new ferns. These clusters are called **sori** (sor' eye). Have you ever seen sori on a fern? If there are ferns near your home, check the underside of the fronds. If they do not have any sori right now, keep checking; they will get them. If you don't have a fern nearby, check your local nursery or discount department store. You will need a frond with sori for the project at the end of this lesson, so try to find one as soon as possible.

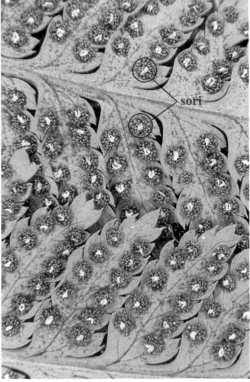

The sori on this fern frond each contain several sporangia, which each contain many spores.

The photograph on the left shows the underside of a fern frond that is full of sori. The little white centers surrounded by brown clumps are the sori. The brown clumps are the sporangia. There are many spores inside the sporangia. Every spore can become a whole new fern if the conditions are right. Now remember, since spores are not seeds, they do not have a food source to help them when they first start to grow. Because of this, a seed is more likely to grow into a plant than is a spore, because the spore needs more ideal conditions than the seed does. Ferns make up for this by producing an *enormous* number of spores. Although most spores will not grow into new ferns, each fern makes so many spores that at least some of them will.

From Spore to Prothallus to Fiddlehead to Fern

So what does a fern spore need to do in order to make a new plant? Well, first the spore must leave its container, the sporangium ("sporangium" is the singular form of "sporangia"). When the spores in a sporangium are ready to leave, the sporangium opens up and flings the spores into the air. The spores float in the air until they land somewhere. If a spore lands somewhere with suitable conditions, it grows into a tiny, heart-shaped plantlet called a **prothallus** (pro thal' us). The prothallus is usually very hard to see because it is small and often lightly-colored or transparent. If you see a bunch of ferns growing in a forest, it is possible that there is a prothallus (perhaps several) growing close by, but you would have to search hard with a magnifying glass to find it.

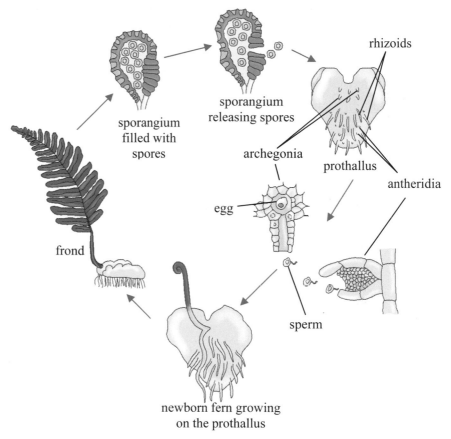

The prothallus is not what we think of when we think of ferns. Nevertheless, it is a part of the way that a spore develops into a fern, so we say that the prothallus is a part of the fern's **lifecycle**. In a way, the prothallus is like a flower, although it's not nearly as pretty as a flower. Instead, it looks like a little heart-shaped, squishy thing with "roots" dangling from its base. Those roots are called **rhizoids** (ry' zoyds), and they absorb water and nutrients from the soil.

The reason a prothallus is like a flower is that it has male and female parts, just like a flower has. The male parts on the prothallus are little bumps on its base, and they are called **antheridia** (an' ther id' ee uh). Do you recognize the first part of that word? Do you remember what the anther on a flower is? It is the male part of the flower. The antheridia are the male parts of the prothallus. They hold the sperm. The female parts of the prothallus are called the **archegonia** (ark' uh guh nee' uh), and they contain the eggs.

Once the antheridia are mature, they release their sperm, which can actually swim! As long as there is a lot of water around, the sperm will swim around, looking for archegonia to enter. If they find one, they will go inside and fertilize the egg. Although the antheridia and archegonia are very close to one another on the prothallus, they mature at different times. Because of this, the sperm from one prothallus rarely fertilize the eggs of the same prothallus. They usually have to find another prothallus in order to fertilize an egg.

Once an egg is fertilized, it can start to grow into what we call a fern. In order to do this, however, it needs food. Do you know where it gets the food? It gets it from the prothallus! Once the egg is fertilized, it develops a "foot" that imbeds itself in the prothallus and pulls nourishment from it. As the new fern begins to develop, it first develops into what is often called a **fiddlehead** (shown in the picture to the right). Can you see why it is called a fiddlehead? It looks like the top of a violin, which is often called a "fiddle." When the fiddlehead is ready, it will unfurl and develop into the beautiful frond that will allow us to recognize the plant as a fern.

This fiddlehead is an immature fern.

Do you see why I wanted you to understand that a spore is definitely not a seed? Think about all of the steps that a spore must go through in order to develop into a new fern. It must first develop into a prothallus. Then, it must release sperm. If the sperm of one prothallus ends up being able to swim and meet an egg from another prothallus, fertilization will occur. The fertilized egg can then start to develop into what we think of as a fern, but only when it starts pulling nutrients from the prothallus that held the egg. This whole process is actually a lot more detailed than how I have explained it here. It is called an "alternation of generations" lifecycle, and you will learn a *lot* more about it when you take biology in high school.

Other Methods of Reproduction

Although the life cycle that I just explained to you is something that all ferns do, there are other ways that ferns can make new fern plants. Ferns can also grow new fern plants by spreading runners, called **rhizomes** (ry' zohms), along the ground. Many plants do this. You learned in previous lessons, for example, that grass and strawberries produce runners that can form new plants. Do you remember what you learned about the new plants formed this way? They are **clones** of the original plant. They have exactly the same DNA as the plant that made the runner. Ferns produced from rhizomes are also clones of the fern than made the rhizome. In some ferns, if a frond leans down and touches its tip into the dirt, it can sprout new ferns that become planted into the ground. This is a bit like rooting a plant in soil. Once again, those new plants are clones of the original. There is one other way that some ferns can reproduce. When some ferns are in their prothallus stage, the prothallus can make a little packet of cells called a **gemma** (jem' uh). The gemma can be carried off by animals or water to form a new prothallus somewhere else. With all of the different ways that ferns can reproduce, is it any wonder that you find them on nearly every forest floor?

Tree Ferns

Tree ferns are giant ferns that look like trees. In fact, tree ferns even have "trunks," but they are not made of wood like normal tree trunks. Instead, tree fern trunks are composed of a mass of roots that intertwine, giving support to the fronds. As you can see from the picture on the right, they look a lot like palm trees and cycads (the gymnosperm you learned about in the previous lesson). When you see tree ferns, you may not be able to tell them from palm trees or cycads. However, if a tree fern happens to be in the right stage of its growth, you might notice some fiddleheads near the top. That would be one way to tell tree ferns apart from palm trees or cycads.

There is a better way to determine whether you are looking at a palm tree, cycad, or tree fern. You can investigate how the plant reproduces. Palm trees reproduce by making coconuts, cycads reproduce by making cones, and tree ferns reproduce with spores.

This may look like a palm tree or a cycad, but it is a tree fern.

What Do You Remember?

Where do you usually find ferns in a forest? Why are they found in these areas? What is a frond? What are the spots sometimes found on the underside of the frond? In the fern life cycle, what is the little structure with male and female plant parts? Can you name the male part? Can you name the female part? What must be present for the sperm to reach the egg? What is the little baby frond that unfurls called? What are some other ways ferns produce new plants? What are tree ferns? How are they different from cycads and palms?

Notebook Activities

Make an illustration that shows the lifecycle of a fern. You can use the illustration on page 147 as a guide. Once you are done with the illustration, write (or dictate) an explanation of the lifecycle in your own words. Also, draw two illustrations of fern fronds. In the first, draw the top side of a frond and point out the rachis and pinnae. In the other illustration, draw the underside of a frond with sori.

If you have any ferns near your home, illustrate them and, by checking a fern field guide, try to learn what kinds of ferns they are. Include that information in your notebook or field guide. You may also collect specimens for your notebook. You can preserve the color of fern fronds by gluing them to paper using white school glue.

Projects
Fern Transfers

You can make beautiful paintings by pressing a fern that has been painted onto a blank sheet of paper. These can even be framed and used as very stylish home décor!

You will need:
- Paper
- Several fern fronds
- Several colors of paint
- A paint brush or sponge

1. Use the paint brush or sponge to paint the entire fern frond on one side.
2. Turn it over onto a piece of paper while the paint is still wet.
3. Place another piece of a paper on top of the frond and carefully pat the entire frond beneath the page.
4. Remove the paper and the fern frond with great care. You will have a beautiful transfer!
5. Do this with other fern fronds and other colors.

Fern Spores

You might not be able to do this project right away, depending on what time of year it is. You need to find a fern frond that has sori on it. If you can't find one outside, you might check a local nursery or department store that has a lawn and garden section. Often, the ferns there will have sori on them.

You will need:
- A fern frond with sori
- A paper towel
- A hardcover book
- A magnifying glass

1. Open the book and cover the right-hand page with the paper towel.
2. Place the frond on top of the paper towel with the sori facing down.
3. Close the book and leave it overnight.
4. The next morning, open the book and remove the frond. You will probably find a fine dust on the paper towel that the frond was touching.
5. Look at the "dust" with a magnifying glass, and you should see that it is made up of thousands of tiny spores. Each of these spores can produce a whole new fern plant.

Lesson 12
Nonvascular Plants

Do you remember the difference between nonvascular and vascular plants? Explain the difference in your own words. While vascular plants have liquid-carrying tubes in their bodies, nonvascular plants do not. Unless you live in an area that has little moisture in the air, you probably have nonvascular plants in your yard. They are probably growing on trees, rocks, and maybe even your house! What plants am I talking about? I am talking about mosses. Botanists put mosses in phylum **Bryophyta** (bry oh fie' tuh). Do you remember what the Greek term **bryo** means? It means **moss**. It makes sense, then, that mosses are in a phylum called Bryophyta, which means "moss plants."

Even though mosses are by far the most common type of nonvascular plant, there are others. Liverworts are nonvascular plants, and they are put in a different phylum from mosses. Hornworts are also nonvascular plants, and they are put in yet another phylum. Nevertheless, as a group,

You can often find moss growing on trees.

nonvascular plants are called **bryophytes**. Even though not all nonvascular plants are mosses, they are still all called "moss plants," because they all have a lot in common with moss.

Because bryophytes don't have stems, roots, and all those other wonderful fluid-carrying features of the vascular plants, they cannot get their water from the ground. After all, roots must send water they absorb from the ground to the other parts of the plant. Without tubes to carry the water, nonvascular plants can't do that. As you learned in Lesson 1, nonvascular plants act like paper towels, absorbing water and nutrients and then letting them soak through to other parts of the plant. Because of this, nonvascular plants can never grow very tall. If they grew tall, water would not be able to soak through to all parts of the plant. That's one big difference between bryophytes and the vascular plants. Bryophytes are, in general, the smallest members of the plant kingdom.

Nonvascular plants are like the vascular plants in one very important way: they both make their own food using chlorophyll, sunlight, water, and carbon dioxide. Do you remember what that process is called? It's called photosynthesis. Since nonvascular plants do photosynthesis, they need chlorophyll, sunlight, water, and carbon dioxide, just as the vascular plants do. Of course, the fact that moss is green should tip you off that it does photosynthesis. The chlorophyll that is used in photosynthesis gives moss its green color.

Moss

Is there any moss growing on trees near your home? Sometimes you will find little patches of moss on the ground, on wooden structures like homes and fences, and even on rocks. Mosses flourish in wet environments. Remember, they do not have roots that can grow in search of water, so they must absorb water directly through their bodies. A wet environment, therefore, is ideal for them. Despite this, you *can* find mosses in very dry climates, even deserts. This is because mosses have the interesting ability to **desiccate** (des' uh kayt). This means that they can dry out for long periods of time without actually dying. Without water, they will turn brown or yellow because they cannot do any photosynthesis, but they will not be dead. Even after a long time without water, as soon as it rains, they will immediately start doing photosynthesis and turn a lush green again.

Moss grows in many places, even on rocks.

Mosses are important to creation in many ways. They provide a place to live for many tiny creatures, and they are useful to birds for building nests. Most animals don't usually eat moss, because it does not have a lot of nutritional value. However, some animals such as bears, deer, and turtles will eat it if they can't find any other kind of food. There is one animal, however, that eats it regularly: the reindeer. Reindeer live in cold climates, and moss has a special chemical that keeps the fluids inside the reindeer from freezing, even on the coldest of days. Moss, then, is a kind of "reindeer antifreeze."

Of course, there is a type of moss that you might be very familiar with: peat moss. Peat moss can absorb a *lot* of water. Because of this, it is used quite a bit as packing material and mulch. It is called "peat moss" because as it grows in the wild, it decomposes into a peat, which is an excellent "soil" in which to grow plants. Peat also burns well when you dry it out. In fact, there are several electric plants in Ireland that burn peat in order to generate electricity.

Reproduction

Take a guess how nonvascular plants reproduce (make new plants). Do you think they grow flowers, like angiosperms? Do you think they make cones, like gymnosperms? Do you think they grow spores, like ferns? All nonvascular plants reproduce like ferns. They produce spores.

Since nonvascular plants produce spores like ferns, you might expect their lifecycles to be complicated, like the fern lifecycle. Well, you would be right. Since mosses are the most common nonvascular plants in creation, I want to use moss reproduction to illustrate how all nonvascular plants make new nonvascular plants.

Tiny moss plants grow from spores that germinate in the ground. The really complex part, however, is how those plants form new spores. You see, there are male mosses and female mosses. Guess what male mosses have. They have little structures called **antheridia**. Do you remember that term from the previous lesson? Can you tell me what a moss's antheridia produce? They produce sperm. Guess what those sperm can do. They can swim, just like fern sperm. Can you tell me what structures female moss plants have? They have **archegonia**, which contain eggs. The sperm from moss antheridia swim to the eggs in moss archegonia so that fertilization can take place.

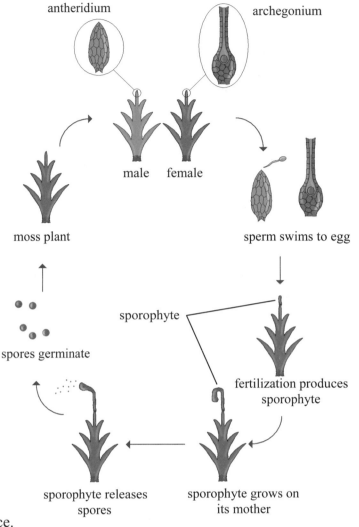

What is produced when the sperm fertilizes the egg? A little stalk called a **sporophyte** (spoor' uh fyt) is produced. The sporophyte grows right on top of the female moss plant, and guess what it produces? It produces the spores that will germinate into moss plants.

The stalks in this picture are sporophytes that are growing on their mother moss plants.

Like ferns, mosses have other ways that they can reproduce. Bits of a single moss plant, if broken off, can grow into a completely new moss plant. Some mosses also produce little structures called **brood bodies**. These structures are designed to be separated from the plant and then grow into a different moss plant. As is the case with ferns, when mosses reproduce in either of these two ways, the new plant is a clone of the original plant.

Liverworts

Liverworts were named in England many years ago. You see, many species of this nonvascular plant have a shape that looks like a person's liver. Thus, people used what was at the time their word for **liver (lifer)** and their word for **plant (wyrt)** to come up with the name **liverwort**. Back in those days, people believed that if a plant was shaped like a certain part of the body, it must help that part of the body. So guess what ancient people used liverworts for? They used them to try to treat diseases of the liver. Of course, today we know that such an idea is not correct. As far as medical science can tell, liverworts have no serious medicinal value.

The shape of these liverworts reminds some of the human liver.

If you want to look for liverworts, look in shaded, moist areas, such as on the ground beneath shrubs or on a shady stream bank. There are two main types of liverworts: **leafy liverworts** and **thallose liverworts**. Leafy liverworts look like leaves on a stem which lies horizontally on the surface of the ground. The "leaves" are most often arranged in two rows, but in many species there is a third row of much smaller "leaves" which can be found with a magnifying glass. Now remember, since these plants do not have vascular tissue, they really don't have leaves and stems. They just form structures that look like leaves and stems. The majority of liverworts are leafy. Thallose liverworts do not appear to have leaves or stems. They tend to look like a mass of flattened or wavy green tissue on the ground.

Lichen

You learned a little bit about **lichens** (like' uns) in Lesson 1. Although lichens are not really plants, they are often discussed with the nonvascular plants, because scientists used to think that they were nonvascular plants. However, after studying lichens for some time, scientists actually came to the conclusion that lichens are really made of up two different kinds of living things: **fungus** and **algae** (al' jee). Do you know what a fungus is? A fungus is a special kind of living thing that feeds off of dead creatures. We call them "decomposers," because they decompose (break down) dead things so that the dead things can be recycled back into creation. A mushroom is an example of a fungus. Algae are microscopic creatures (which means they are too tiny to see with just our eyes) that typically live in water.

When the fungus and algae meet, if they are a good match and conditions are right, they will form a union and create lichen! The fungus forms the body, while the algae make the food by

photosynthesis. They are a good pair, aren't they? When two different organisms form a relationship where they are dependent on one another, it is called **symbiosis** (sim by oh' sis). Lichen is an example of symbiosis between algae and fungus. Can you think of another example of symbiosis that we have discussed in this book? Remember the process of pollination? Flowering plants (angiosperms) and their pollinators live in symbiosis. The plants provide food (nectar) for the pollinators, and the pollinators help the plants reproduce.

Lichens come in all shapes, sizes, and colors. They can look like a rust-colored dye that has been painted onto a rock or tree; a scalloped, wrinkled gray or green sheet; lacey pads; bushy clumps; chaotic strands of black, gray, or green "hair;" even branching, tiny, gray structures that look like deer antlers! The most common lichen is the kind found on trees. It is usually green or gray and looks like wrinkled

The orange, green, yellow, and gray splotches on these rocks are lichens.

leaves growing on the trunk of the tree. If you look hard, you can probably find lichens growing near your home.

In some environments, lichens can literally cover a tree trunk and all its branches. Believe it or not, this does not harm the tree at all. You see, even though the lichens are growing on the tree, they are not taking anything from the tree. They do not need to take food from the tree, because the algae part of the lichen makes the food. They do not even take water from the tree. They absorb water from the air, and they absorb the rain that falls on them. If anything, the lichens help the tree by giving it another layer of protection besides its bark.

When lichens are wet from rain or dew, they grow actively. If they dry out, they stop growing. Like mosses, however, lichens do not die when they dry up. They just lie dormant until the next rain starts it growing again. Do you remember where the word dormant comes from? It comes from the Latin word that means sleep. Lichen, then, just "sleep" when they are dry.

Lichens cover nearly every inch of this tree trunk.

Pollution Monitors

Remember, lichens absorb water in the air, as well as rainwater, directly through their tissues. They do not use roots that are imbedded into the ground. As a result, they tend to absorb not only the water, but anything that happens to be dissolved in the water as well, including any pollution that might be there. When the air around lichens is clean, the lichens thrive, but when the air is filled with too much pollution, the lichens cannot grow and will become grayish or even black. Often the lichens will simply die off as the air becomes more and more polluted. A city with very poor air quality will have few lichens on the trees.

There are so many different kinds of pollution that scientists and engineers spend a lot of time designing and building devices that measure how clean the air is. More than a hundred years ago, however, a Finnish scientist named William Nylander noticed that lichens on trees in the country around Paris were not found on the trees within the city. He assumed that if they grew in the country around Paris, they should grow in the city as well, so he reasoned that they must have been killed by the air pollution from all the new factories in Paris.

Lichen can be a good indicator of how much pollution is in the air.

These days, we understand that lichens are, indeed, a great measure of air quality. Since they tend to soak up everything that is dissolved in the water that touches them, even pollutants, they are very sensitive to pollution in the air. When there are too many harmful chemicals in the air, lichens die. If you live where there are many lichens, it probably means the air around you is pretty clean. If there are only a few lichens in your neighborhood, the air you are breathing is probably not as clean as lichens like it.

Uses for Lichen

In addition to helping protect trees and giving people a good monitor of our air quality, lichens are important to our environment, just as other plants are. Over a long time, they will break down the rocks upon which they grow, which leads to fresh soil. They are a source of food for both caribou and reindeer. They also become homes for spiders, mites, lice, and other insects. Hummingbirds even use lichen (along with other things like moss and spider webs) to build their nests.

People have learned to use lichens as well. Because lichens come in many different colors, people use them to make dyes for fabric. People eat some varieties of lichens, although other varieties are poisonous. One species of lichen, called "wolf lichen," was actually used by Native Americans to poison wolves. They also used it to make poison in which they could dip their arrowheads. Some lichens have been used by Native Americans as medicine, and recent studies have shown that they do, indeed, contain antibiotic chemicals that help in the treatment of certain kinds of infections.

Lichens grow very slowly, usually less than one inch in a whole year. If you find lichen upon a branch that has fallen, you may collect some for your notebook, but it is best not to peel it off of a tree.

Notebook Activities

Make an illustration of the moss lifecycle for your notebook, using the drawing on p. 153 as a guide. Explain the entire lifecycle. Write down all that you remember about moss, lichen and liverworts in your notebook. Draw an illustration of each one.

If you live in an area where moss, liverworts and lichen grow well, go outside and study them. Use a field guide to try to identify the ones growing in your area, and include information about them in the field guide that you are making.

Project
Test Your Air with a Lichenometer

You will need:
♦ A coat hanger
♦ Yarn
♦ Tape
♦ Trees with lichen on them, preferably in different places (Lichens prefer oak trees as they can keep the water locked into the deep ridges of the oak bark better than in the bark of most trees.)

If you live in a climate that has some regular moisture in the air, you will be able to tell how clean the air is in your area by the rate of lichen growth on the trees. In order to do this, you must first make a "lichenometer."

1. Bend the hook of the coat hanger until it forms an oval, and then cover it with tape for safety.
2. Bend the entire coat hanger into a long oval or rectangle shape.

3. Cut several pieces of yarn about 10 inches long.
4. Cut three pieces of yarn about 20 inches long.
5. Begin tying the yarn across the bent coat hanger to make a series of squares out of the yarn (see the picture on the right).
6. The end product should resemble a tennis racket. (Of course, if you have an old tennis racket, you could just use that instead.)

Now that you have made your "lichenometer," you can use it to measure the amount of lichen on trees in various locations. Look for a particular type of tree (oak trees are best) that appear in lots of different places in your area of the country. Find the place on the tree with the most lichen growth and place the lichenometer over that area. Count the number of squares that are completely filled with lichen. If a square is only partly filled with lichen, don't count it. Take the number of squares that are completely filled with lichen and divide by the total number of squares on your lichenometer. Then, multiply by 100. The result will be the percentage of your lichenometer that was filled with lichen. For example, if my lichenometer had 40 squares in it and 16 of them were completely filled with lichen, the percentage would be:

$$16 \div 40 \times 100 = 40\%$$

Older Students: You can make a science fair project out of this! Use your lichenometer to test the lichen growth from trees in the city compared to trees in the country. Look for parks in the city and woody areas in the country. Your hypothesis might be that the further you get from the city, the higher the percentage of lichen on the trees. If your hypothesis is supported by your testing, the reason could be that the air is cleaner the farther you get from the city.

You will want to collect limbs that have fallen from trees to display on your tri-fold board. The limbs from the city may only have a small patch of lichen, while the limbs from the country may be virtually covered with lichen. The closer you are to a highway, the less lichen you may find as well. To make your project scientifically accurate, measure the same number of trees in each area that you study. That way, you will be treating each area with the same level of scrutiny. Use the same type of trees in all areas also, because lichens grow better on some trees than others. After all, if you find a difference in lichen growth, you don't want it to be because you looked at different types of trees!

Lesson 13
Nature Journaling

"As soon as he is able to keep it himself, a nature diary is a source of delight to a child. Every day's walk gives him something to enter." - Charlotte Mason [The Original Homeschooling series Vol. 1, p. 54 – retrieved from http://mywebpages.comcast.net/leslienoelani/toc.html on 07/19/2004]

Now that you have completed your study of the amazing Kingdom Plantae, you will want to keep growing in your knowledge and wonder of nature by keeping nature journals. What are nature journals? They are simply books that you make yourself. In them, you illustrate and record your discoveries, thoughts, and observations in the great outdoors.

Field biologists are scientists that spend time outdoors studying nature. They often keep nature journals, as have many great scientists from the past. They use their nature journals to record their observations and write down their thoughts. When you are nature journaling outside, it is a time to be quiet and still. It is a time to allow your thoughts to focus on those things that are around you. It is a time to slow down and enjoy God's creation. It is a time for thinking, or as we often say, reflection.

Many famous explorers and scientists were dedicated to nature journaling. Christopher Columbus kept a detailed log, or journal, of his travels. Lewis and Clark diligently kept nature journals, recording all the wonderful and amazing plants and animals they encountered on their expedition across America.

This is a portion of Meriwether Lewis's nature journal.

John James Audubon was a famous naturalist (a person who studies nature) who traveled far and wide to study, sketch, and eventually paint the wildlife and plants he found in nature. He mostly focused on birds. That is why groups that study birds are often called Audubon groups. Even today, in museums across the world, you can see John James Audubon's drawings and paintings of the many birds and animals he studied.

Do you think John James Audubon or any of the great illustrators of field guides began drawing nature as an expert? No, they began as beginners, as we all do, and as you probably are today. With practice and time, however, they became very famous for their work.

We always start nature study and nature journaling as beginners. With dedication to the task, our entire family can become experts: mom, dad, and all the kids can keep nature journals. Great minds, like those of the naturalists of the past, are trained through careful and quiet study. Nature journaling is one way that you can train your mind to think like a scientist!

Field biologists and naturalists teach themselves to notice details in the different **flora** and **fauna** they see. The word "flora" is a general word that means "plant life," while "fauna" is a general word that means "animal life." We can do this as well. From flowers, trees, and lichen to birds, squirrels, and insects, there is so much to learn from just watching and thinking about what we see. After all, nature is the best science classroom! It teaches us the wonderful and important skill of observation, and it also gives us pleasure and enjoyment that indoor studies simply cannot provide.

This is a John James Audubon drawing of mallard ducks.

How do we go about nature study and nature journaling? We can simply begin in our own neighborhoods. I must give you a word of warning, however. Going outside with our pencils and journals may seem exciting at first, but before we have really learned how to observe and notice the details around us, we may tire of it quickly. The entire process of learning to keep a nature journal requires us to be silent, still, and thoughtful. This is something that people long ago did often. Today, many of us have lost the wonderful skill of being still and contemplative (thinking deeply about God's creation). However, if we persevere in the habit of a weekly journey outdoors, we will soon find that our minds have matured, our thoughts have matured, and our observation skills have grown.

The attention to detail that we can learn through nature journaling will benefit us greatly in every area of our lives. Continuing our nature study, even when it seems to be dull, will bring profits that are hard to measure right now. In the future, however, you will look back and see that it yielded

amazing results! When we first start nature study, we will not notice much, except the most obvious signs around us. As we become more accustomed to noticing even the slightest details and changes, however, we will begin to think like scientists. Even if you don't plan on becoming a scientist, these skills will bless you in whatever you do. You will be glad you started and continued with your journaling. Training our eyes to see, teaching our ears to hear, and schooling our minds to be still are just some of the great benefits of nature study.

Though I recommend beginning your journal with your observations and thoughts in your own neighborhood, you will want to take your nature journal on every walk or outdoor activity you attend. You will want your nature journal to be small enough to fit inside a small sack, back pack, or even your pocket. This will make it easier to take it on hikes and through nature trails, or even to your local park. It's also helpful to have a place where you can keep a pencil or a pack of colored pencils.

At the end of this lesson, you will make your own nature journal. This will be the first of many that you will create for your future studies. You can make them as simple or as elaborate as you wish. In these journals, you can include anything you think is noteworthy.

Since you have learned a lot about plants this year, you will want to include anything that is interesting about the flora you find outside. You can draw pictures, write down your thoughts, and even write down what you remember learning from this book. For example, if you see bright green lichen completely covering a tree, you can write down that lichen is greener where the air quality is good, which is something you learned from this book. You may also want to write down that lichen only grows about an inch per year, taking note that the lichen on that particular tree has been growing a great many years since it is so full. You can draw a picture of the lichen tree next to your notes.

You don't have to worry if your handwriting is not very good or your drawing isn't perfect! The only way to get better at drawing is by drawing and drawing and drawing some more. You will be happy to see the results if you keep trying to draw what you see every week as you go out on your nature walk. Eventually, what you draw will look almost exactly like what you see.

A nature journal will include all that you see in nature, including all the animals you find. You can sketch or draw the wildlife, writing down the colors or using colored pencils if you have them.

When you get home, you can use more colors as you remember them, and you can look on the internet or in a field guide to discover what animals you saw. It's great to have field guides at home to identify the wildlife you see and study. It might also be fun to get a book on how to draw animals. This will help you to improve your illustration skills more quickly.

In the next few pages, we will explore the different kinds of information you may want to include in your nature journal. These journals will provide you with memories and information that you will find fascinating in the years to come. When you are an adult, you will love to look over your past journals as they will bring a flood of memories from your days as a scientist in training.

This is a John James Audubon drawing of cardinals.

Where and When

Because this is a journal, it is very important to *always* include the date, time, and location of your experience. This will prove to be very important to you in the future. When you look back over your old journals, you will want to know what year, season, and time of day it was that you encountered the things you recorded. It is helpful to get a small calendar from a checkbook register and tape it to the inside cover page of your journal.

Recording the location is also of vital importance. This is a great way to keep scientific records. Suppose you see a cardinal outside. If you write down the time, date, and location, you may find that the next year, on the exact same date, you will see the cardinal again. As time goes on, you might learn that the cardinal keeps to a schedule. That will tell you something about patterns in the cardinal's behavior. It would be quite frustrating to look for patterns like that only to discover that you forgot to record the date, time, and location when you were making your observations.

Illustrations

Illustrations are an attempt to accurately draw something you see in nature. You can illustrate one thing, such as one flower on an entire bush of flowers, or the entire scene that you see, such as a waterfall and all the rocks and trees around it.

Taking colored pencils on your nature walk makes it more enjoyable and easier to record the correct colors and patterns on the animals and plants you see. However, everyone, including mom, will need to take his or her time, relax, and be willing to spend a long time in one spot to get some good colored illustrations. We tend to be in a hurry, even when we are out in nature, but a natural setting is a wonderful place to take our time, sit and think, and slowly draw and enjoy the beautiful world that God made.

You will sometimes want to leave some room for writing words or descriptions around your illustrations. Other times, you may want to fill up the entire page with your illustration and write the words, descriptions, time, date, and place on the page before or after it. Not every page in your nature journal has to have a drawing or anything pictured on it. Sometimes, you will just write down what you see or think.

Sketches with Labels

Sketches are a little different than illustrations. They are often drawn more quickly with only one color pencil or pen. They will often have labels with arrows pointing to different parts of the sketch. Sometimes, you may not feel like making an elaborate illustration of your observations. On these days, a simple sketch will be preferred. This is your journal. Whatever you choose to do is great.

Lists

Sometimes it is helpful to make lists of things you see in nature. You can just simply write down every kind of tree you see on your nature walk through a certain park, or you may want to record the name of every bird that comes into your back yard on a particular day.

Lists will prove to be an interesting and important aspect of scientific study. With lists, you can begin to notice things that change in your area. Perhaps you remember always seeing a certain flower or bird in the spring, but later on you find that it isn't present anymore. These are the kinds of observations that genuine scientists make.

Descriptions

Of course, you will want to include lots of descriptions of the wildlife you encounter in your nature journal. Writing down the colors, shapes, and everything else you notice will be important to you. How does everything look today? Every season has its own special features. An assortment of animals and insects inhabits your area during different months. The plants look completely different in the fall compared to the spring. What was once a bush full of beautiful blue flowers covered with bumblebees becomes a bush full of red berries with many visiting birds. Keeping records of these things is very important for scientific study.

You will also want to describe the weather on each day that you are studying nature. All of this will help to bring back the exact memory when you read over your journal in years to come. In their nature journals, biologists take specific notes about each species of animal or plant they see. Their journals are filled with detailed information about what they are studying.

You can learn to record this kind of detail yourself. When you are nature journaling, begin by giving information about the weather and the setting. Then, pick something to study that is very

specific, like a patch of clover. After you have decided what to study, ask yourself questions about it. What does it look like? Does it have any special features that seem interesting or different than other plants or animals? If it is a plant; can you identify the leaf venation, shape, and margin? What is the color of its leaves? Are there flowers? What do they look like? Can you tell whether it is a monocot or a dicot? Look closer with a magnifying glass. Is there anything else special about it that you notice? Don't worry about knowing the names of the plants or animals. You can learn those when you get home. Your detailed notes will be very special and important to you as you continue your studies of nature. This is also the best way to train your mind in observation and attention to detail.

Your Own Poetry or Songs

When we are outside, with all of God's creation surrounding us, sometimes we might think of our own special verses or thoughts about the things we see. Many great poems and songs have been written while people were enjoying nature. Poetry and songs come from our heart, but learning to express your thoughts this way takes practice. A great way to begin is to start using forms of expression called **similes, metaphors,** and **personifications**. These forms of expression are almost always used in poetry and songs.

A simile is an expression that compares two things which are in no way alike using a connecting word, such as "like." For example, consider the phrase, "Reckless words pierce like a sword." This is a simile because two unlike things (reckless words and a sword) are being compared to each other using the connective word "like."

A metaphor also compares two unlike things. However, metaphors do not use a connective word in the comparison. When a writer creates a metaphor, he is actually stating that something is something else. For example, the phrase, "You are the salt of the earth" is a metaphor. Two unlike things (you and salt) are being directly compared without using a connective word. This metaphor is saying that you are an important element of the earth that makes it better. Just as salt makes food taste better, you make the earth a better place.

When you use personification, you are giving the qualities of a person to a thing or an idea. In other words, you are talking about a nonhuman thing as if it were a person. For example, the phrase

"The tree's branches wore lichen like a coat" is a personification of a tree. After all, the tree is described as possessing the human ability of being able to wear something.

The easiest way to come up with one of these expressions is to imagine if *you* were that bird, flower, or tree. How would you describe what you were doing? How would you feel? What would you think of the things surrounding you? You may want to read some poetry to help you imagine how things can be described using these three kinds of expressions.

It may be easy for some people to write with similes, metaphors, and personifications, but others may find it very difficult. With practice, however, everyone can write poetry in his or her nature journal. You may want to begin with one or two sentences to describe something. You could write something like, "The tree showed off his lichen coat to all the animals of the forest." With time, you will begin to think of different similes, metaphors, and personifications when you are out in nature.

Poetry or Songs You Know

Writing poetry and songs that you make up is a wonderful thing to add to your notebook, but it's also a good idea to write down poems or parts of a song that you think of when you are outside. For example, when you are out in nature and see the little animals scurry by, you may be reminded of the hymn, "All Creatures Great and Small." You can write down a verse from a song or you can simply write the title of the song as you illustrate the beauty and wildlife that you see.

God's creation can inspire us to remember songs we love.

Remember that this is your journal. It's an expression of your thoughts, ideas and musings. There is no right way or wrong way to do it. Feel free to write anything you think of as you experience nature.

Scripture and Prayer

One of the most beautiful ways to express your appreciation to God for the wonderful world He has given us is to read, remember, and write Scriptures when you are experiencing nature. The Psalms are filled with praises and songs that highlight God's work. Often, if you take a small Bible with you, you can find a Psalm that perfectly describes the way you feel when you are outdoors enjoying the world God fashioned.

It's also special to include prayers that you may have in your journal. This nature journal will be a reflection of the person that you are today; the hopes and needs that you have now. Later on, it will be a blessing to look over the prayers and Scriptures that were important to you and to see how God has been faithful to you through the years.

Thoughts

You will also want to include your thoughts in your journal. Include your feelings, hopes, ideas, and dreams. You will want to remember these things as you get older. It's always a joy to read back over the thoughts and ideas you had during this time in your life. You will look back and realize that some of your hopes and dreams have actually come true! You will also see how God has matured you and changed your hopes and dreams into things that are different. Recording all of these things can be very personal and special to you. They will make your nature journal a very important part of you.

What Do You Remember?

Who are some famous people that kept journals? What kinds of things will you put in your nature journal? What can you do with your nature journal once you get older?

Project
Make a Nature Journal

You will need:

◆ Glue

◆ Plain white paper

◆ A cereal box

◆ Yarn or ribbon

◆ A hole puncher

◆ Fabric or construction paper for the cover

◆ A pencil

Instructions

1. Begin by cutting out two rectangles of equal size from the cereal box. These two pieces of cardboard will serve as the back and front covers of your nature journal. Remember to think of the size of your nature journal when you cut the two rectangles. If you make them too large, the nature journal will be hard to carry on hikes and nature walks. Of course, if you make your journal too small, it will be hard to put much information in it.

2. Cut the plain white paper into rectangles that are just a little smaller than the covers you cut in step #1. You will want to have several pages, because you will want to fill your nature journal with a lot of information.

3. Use the hole puncher to punch two holes into the cardboard covers, making certain that the holes line up when you put the two pieces of cardboard together.

4. Use the hole puncher to punch holes in every sheet of paper, making certain they line up with the holes in the cardboard covers.

5. Cover the outside cardboard covers with fabric or construction paper. Use glue to attach the fabric or construction paper to the covers.

6. Use the hole puncher to punch holes through the fabric or construction paper right where the holes are in the cardboard.

7. Stack the papers in between the covers so that all of the punched holes line up.

8. Cut a long piece of yarn.

9. Use the pencil to guide the yarn through the top hole, and then guide the same end of the yarn through the bottom hole.

10. Tie the yarn so that it holds the nature journal together. Do not tie it too tightly, or the paper will rip when the pages are turned.

Answers to the Narrative Questions

Your child should not be expected to know the answer to every question. These questions are designed to jog the child's memory and help him put the concepts into his own words. *The questions are highlighted in bold and italic type*. The answers are in plain type.

Lesson 1

What is biology? The study of living things. ***What is botany?*** The study of plants. ***Are all botanists biologists?*** Yes. ***Are all biologists botanists?*** No. ***Why do scientists use Latin?*** It allows people from different countries to have common names for the things they are studying, and it doesn't change. ***What is taxonomy?*** The process of classifying things. ***What is binomial nomenclature?*** Using two names (genus and species) for a living thing. ***Sample Shoe Taxonomy System:*** Kingdoms: work shoes, play shoes, dress shoes, slippers; Phyla: boots, regular shoes; Classes: shoes with laces, shoes without laces; Families: hard soles, soft soles; Genera: open-toed, closed-toed; Species: shoe *color*. ***Pause a moment and explain in your own words what makes a plant a vascular plant.*** A vascular plant has tubes inside it. ***What does the vascular system of a plant do?*** Carry water and other chemicals. ***What does your vascular system do?*** Carries blood. ***What else have you learned so far?*** The tubes in plants are xylem and phloem, and the main vein in a leaf is the midrib. ***Can you tell someone in your own words what angiosperms are?*** Plants that make flowers. ***What does angiosperm mean?*** Seed container. ***In which phylum do botanists put the angiosperms?*** Phylum Anthophyta. ***What does the name of the phylum mean?*** Flower plant. ***What is the purpose of a flower?*** To make seeds. ***Name something you remember about angiosperms.*** They make flowers. ***What are gymnosperms?*** Plants that make cones. ***What does the word "coniferophyta" mean?*** Cone-bearing plant. ***What do ferns and mosses have in common?*** They make sporangia. ***What is different between ferns and mosses?*** Ferns are vascular, mosses are not. ***What is the phylum for ferns?*** Phylum Pterophyta. ***What is the phylum for mosses?*** Phylum Bryophyta.

Lesson 2

What is a seed? It is a baby plant in a protective coating with food. ***What does "dormant" mean?*** Asleep. ***What does a seed need to wake up and begin growing?*** Warmth, water, and air. ***What is the baby plant in a seed called?*** An embryo. ***What is the seed's testa?*** The seed's coat. ***What does it do?*** Protects the embryo. ***What is the hilum on a seed?*** The scar from where it was attached to its mother. ***Describe germination.*** The student should give the steps outlined in the drawing on page 27. ***What is the top part of the embryo called?*** Epicotyl. ***What are the feather-like leaves on the embryo called?*** Plumules. ***What is the embryo's root called?*** The radicle. ***What is the nutrition within the seed called before it gets absorbed by the cotyledons?*** Endosperm. ***What is the testa?*** Seed coat. ***Explain how the testa comes off for germination.*** When it absorbs water, it loosens to let the water into the seed. ***What is a producer?*** A living thing that makes its own food. ***What is a consumer?*** A living thing that eats other living things for food. ***Are plants producers or consumers?*** Producers. ***Are people producers or consumers?*** Consumers. ***Plant Identification Activity:*** A. dicot (4 petals) B. Monocot (6 petals) C. Monocot (parallel veins) D. Dicot (branched veins)

Lesson 3

What is so special about angiosperms? They make beautiful flowers and provide food for lots of creation. *What is the purpose of a flower?* To make seeds. *What is the job of the sepal?* To protect the bud. *What are all of the sepals together called?* The calyx. *Explain what the corolla is.* It is all of the petals together. *What is the nutrient that carnivorous plants use from the creatures they digest?* Nitrogen. *How does a Venus flytrap keep from shutting its leaf when something other than an animal falls into its trap?* Something must touch two of its hairs, one after the other. *Describe the bladderwort and how it traps its prey.* It has bladders on its roots that open up when an insect or fish hits them and then sucks the insect or fish into the bladders. *Why is the pitcher plant the most frightening of the carnivorous plants?* It is known to trap and digest the largest animals. *Explain why creatures trapped in the pitcher plant cannot escape it.* It has tiny prickles pointing down that poke the insect that is trying to crawl up the sides. It also has rainwater in it that drowns the insect. *Explain how sundews trap and digest animals.* They are covered with sticky goo that makes the insect stick to the plant. When the insect is stuck, they wrap tentacles around the insect to keep it trapped.

Lesson 4

What was the most interesting thing you learned today? The answer to this question will obviously depend on the student. *What would you like to remember of all that you learned?* Once again, this depends on the student. *Explain wind pollination and self-pollination to someone else.* Wind pollination is when pollen floats on the wind until it lands on the carpel of a flower. It is very inefficient, so wind-pollinated plants must make a lot of pollen. Self-pollination is when the pollen from a flower lands on the carpel of a flower of the same plant. *Can you also explain why a flower petal dries up and falls off after it has been pollinated?* There are two reasons. The flower needs to spend its energy making the seeds, and the flower no longer needs to attract pollinators.

Lesson 5

What is the main purpose of fruits? They help disperse seeds. *What is the difference between a fruit and a vegetable?* A fruit contains seeds. A vegetable does not. *Describe what seed dispersal means.* It means moving the seed away from its mother plant. *Explain the two methods of dispersal that we have discussed so far.* Human dispersal is where humans move seeds around to plant crops. Water dispersal is where seeds float on water to move away from their mother plants. *Which Flies Farthest Project*: Usually, the samara will fly farther. Because it is heavier, it is less affected by air resistance. Your results may be different, however, depending on the conditions under which you did the experiment.

Lesson 6

Why are the leaves of a plant so important? They make the food for the plant. *Can you explain to someone what the stomata do for a plant?* They open and close, allowing carbon dioxide in and oxygen out. *Explain what would happen if a plant lost all its leaves.* It would die of starvation. *What does a plant take in from the air and what does it put back into the air?* It takes in carbon dioxide and puts oxygen into the air. *Can you explain photosynthesis in your own words?* It is the process by which plants combine water and oxygen, use light's energy that is absorbed by chlorophyll, and make sugar and oxygen. *Can you remember the four things a plant needs to make food?* Water, carbon dioxide, light, and chlorophyll. *What kind of food does the plant make?* Sugar. *What happens when one ingredient is removed?* Photosynthesis can't happen. *What makes leaves green?* Chlorophyll.)*Testing a Hypothesis Activity:* If the student is testing for light, he must keep at least two plants: one that gets light and one that does not. He should take great care to keep light away from the plant that doesn't get light. He should water and check on both plants when it is dark, for example. If he is testing for water, he should grow the plants side-by-side, with the only difference being that one does not get water. Eventually, the plant not getting light or not getting water should die. Some plants are hardier than others, so this could take a long time. Ferns are not good plants to use for the water experiment. *Testing Transpiration Project:* In this experiment, the student should eventually see water droplets (from water that transpired through the leaf) in the plastic bag.

Lesson 7

What are the three main purposes for roots? They anchor the plant to the ground, absorb water and nutrients for the plant, and help to prevent erosion. *Explain why root hairs are important.* They do most of the work of absorbing water and nutrients. *What is the root cap?* It is the strongest part of the root, right at the tip. *Where do roots add to their length?* At their tips. *What are the roots always looking for?* Water and nutrients. *What is geotropism?* The ability of plant roots to grow down into the earth. *What is another name for geotropism?* Gravotropism. *Taproot Project:* The carrot in the blue water should sprout new secondary roots, and when you cut it open, you should see blue streaks inside. That's because the carrot (being a root) sucked up the water. The carrot in the refrigerator should not have secondary roots and should not be blue.

Lesson 8

Celery Experiment: After soaking for just a little while, you should see dots on the bottom of the celery stalk where the xylem pulled up colored water. After 24 hours or so, you should see the leaves on the celery starting to turn the color of the water, because the colored water was pulled all the way up to the leaves. *Seeking the Light Project:* The plant in the cup with the lid should end up growing down towards the hole through which light is shining. The other plant should grow straight up.

Lesson 9

What are some reasons God made trees? They help make oxygen for us; they limit erosion; they provide shade for us and shelter for animals. They also provide food for some animals. *How can you tell how much a tree has grown by its branch?* Look for the distance between the terminal bud scars. *Explain the anatomy of a twig. Be sure to include terminal buds, lenticels, nodes, internodes, and auxiliary buds in your explanation.* A twig has a terminal bud on its end, auxiliary buds on its sides, lenticels along its side to help it breathe, nodes where the auxiliary buds form, and scars from the previous years' terminal buds.

Lesson 10

Where are the largest trees in the world found? In the state of California. *What kind of trees are they?* Giant sequoias, which could also be called redwoods. *Where are the oldest trees in the world found?* In the state of California. *What kind of trees are they?* Bristlecone pines. *What is the name of the oldest tree in the world?* Methuselah. *How does it provide evidence for the account of the worldwide Flood reported in the Bible?* It is only about 4,700 years old, which is roughly when the worldwide Flood occurred. If the Flood did not occur, we would find trees *much* older than that. *Comparing Transpiration Activity:* In this experiment, the bag around the conifer needles should have the least amount of water in it. ***What are the three kinds of leaves that conifers can have?*** Needle-like, awl-like, and scale-like. ***What is the process by which conifers produce seeds?*** They produce pollen cones and seed cones. When the pollen cones release their pollen, if it reaches a seed cone, fertilization occurs and seeds develop. ***How long does it take for an egg to be fertilized?*** A year. ***How can forest fires be beneficial to a forest?*** The burned trees fertilize the soil, and the cleared landscape can host a larger variety of living things. ***Name two conifers that don't produce cones.*** Junipers and yews. ***Why are cycads considered gymnosperms?*** Because they produce cones rather than fruits. ***Describe a cycad.*** It looks like a palm, but it produces cones. ***Describe the ginkgo.*** It looks like an angiosperm, because its leaves are broad and fall off before winter. ***Why are ginkgos considered gymnosperms?*** They produce uncovered seeds. ***What are some differences between them and other gymnosperms?*** Cycads have wood and leaves like those of angiosperms, and ginkgos have leaves that are like angiosperm leaves. ***Why do people prefer to plant the male Ginkgo biloba?*** The female ginkgo makes seeds, and when the seed coats come off, they smell terrible. ***Opening and Closing Pinecones Project:*** When the pinecone is put in the cold water, it should close up, because pinecones are designed to open only on hot, dry days. When put in the oven, however, it should open up, because it is hot and dry in the oven.

Lesson 11

Where do you usually find ferns in a forest? On the forest floor, in the shade. ***Why are they found in these areas?*** They like very moist environments. ***What is a frond?*** A fern leaf. ***What are the spots sometimes found on the underside of the frond?*** Sori, which are groups of sporangia. ***In the fern life cycle, what is the little structure with male and female plant parts?*** *The prothallus.* ***Can you name the male part?*** Antheridia. ***Can you name the female part?*** Archegonia. ***What must be present for the sperm to reach the egg?*** Water. ***What is the little baby frond that unfurls called?*** A fiddlehead. ***What are some other ways ferns produce new plants?*** They can produce runners to root a new fern, and some leaves can produce a new fern if they touch the soil. The prothallus can also make a gemma. ***What are tree ferns?*** Large ferns that look like palm trees. ***How are they different from cycads and palms?*** The trunks are not made of wood, and they reproduce with spores. At certain times, they also have fiddleheads.

Lesson 12

There are no narrative questions in this lesson.

Lesson 13

Who are some famous people that kept journals? Columbus, Lewis and Clark, Audubon. ***What kinds of things will you put in your nature journal?*** The answer to this question depends on the student. ***What can you do with your nature journal once you get older?*** You can look back and remember your younger days. You can also see how God has been faithful to you, how He answered your prayers, and how you matured over the years.

Photograph and Illustration Credits

Photos and illustrations from www.clipart.com: 1-2 (all), 3 (drawing), 5-7 (all), 10 (paper towels), 11 (both), 12 (apple and cactus), 13 (both), 15-16 (all), 18 (bottom), 20-21, 22 (bottom), 23 (drawing and coconut), 25-26, 32 (photos marked "C" and "D"), 33 (both), 34 (scissors), 35, 36 (drawings), 37 (boy), 42 (all), 59 (top), 61 (bottom), 64 (top), 66, 67 (right), 72 (top), 74 (top), 75 (bottom), 76 (bottom), 77 (top), 79 (both), 80 (bottom), 81 (all), 82 (all but the bottom two), 83 (all), 87 (bottom). 94 (middle), 95 (middle), 96, 102 (both middle and bottom left), 107 (both), 108 (bottom), 111-112 (all), 113 (top two), 116, 121, 125 (top), 128 (bottom), 135 (bottom), 137, 139 (top left), 140 (bottom), 141 (top), 151, 162, 163, 166 (top)

Photos and Illustrations courtesy NASA/JPL/Caltech: 3 (skylab)

Photos by Kathleen J. Wile: 4, 10 (moss/lichen), 23 (seeds), 39, 59 (bottom), 65, 71 (bottom), 97 (both bottom), 98 (all three on bottom), 108 (top), 109, 110 (bottom), 113 (bottom), 117 (both), 120 (bottom), 122 (top two), 146 (top), 152, 155 (top), 165

Illustrations by Megan Whitaker: 8, 24, 27-28, 40 (carpel), 41 (top), 44 (bottom), 48 (top), 51 (top), 56 (bottom), 60 (both), 73, 82 (bottom two), 84, 87 (top), 88 (top), 91, 94 (top), 97 (top), 98 (top), 99-101 (all), 102 (top), 118, 119 (top), 123, 129, 132, 147, 153 (top)

Photos copyright © Corel Corporation: 9 (flowers), 12 (top), 31 (right), 32 (all except "C" and "D"), 36 (flowers), 40 (all flowers), 53 (lady slipper), 54, 55, 57 (both), 62 (bottom), 64 (bottom), 67 (left), 133

Photos copyright © Corbis Corporation: 9 (leaf), 128 (top), 135 (top)

Photos copyright © Brand X Pictures: 14 (top), 22 (top), 41 (bottom)

Photos copyright © Photodisc, Inc.: 14 (top), 125 (bottom), 139 (top middle), 153 (bottom), 155 (bottom)

Photos by Jeannie K. Fulbright: 17 (both), 18 (top), 48 (bottom), 85, 103, 105, 114, 124 (all), 134, 158 (both), 159 (top), 160 (bottom), 166 (bottom), 167 (both)

Photo copyright © John Foxx Images and Images 4 Communication: 37 (sunflower)

Photos copyright © Painet Photographic Arts and Illustration NETwork: 43, 44 (top), 45-47, 52, 62 (top), 63 (both), 75 (top), 136, 142-143, 146 (bottom), 154

Photos from www.dreamstime.com (copyright © holder in parentheses): 49 (Serban Enache), 50 (bottom-Kathy Dyer), 51 (bottom-Mark Bond), 53 (bee and flower-Serban Enache), 56 (top-Dawn Hudson), 61 (top-Christina Craft), 69 (Newton Page), 71 (top-Scott Rothstein), 74 (middle-Christina Craft), 119 (bottom-Serban Enache)

Photos copyright © Creatas: 50 (top), 149

Photos copyright © Bob Ford/Nature Portfolio: 53 (bee orchid),

Photos by Theresa Pitts-Singer, courtesy of USDA Forest Service, Athens, GA: 58 (all)

Photos copyright © Sotockbyte: 72 (bottom)

Photos copyright © Digital Stock: 74 (bottom), 139 (bottom)

Photos from www.istockphoto.com (copyright © holder in parentheses): 31 (left- Karen Grotzinger), 76 (top- Lanica Klein), 77 (bottom-Li Cat), 78 (Bryan Weinstein), 80 (top-Thierry Arnould), 88 (bottom-Amanda Rohde), 89 (Kaycee Craig), 90 (Rob Sylvan), 94 (bottom-Daniel Chamberlain), 95 (top- Scott Waite), 102 (bottom right-Adam Homfray), 104 (Andrzej Tokarski), 106 (Ben Walker), 110 (top- Nicola Stratford), 120 (top-David Dycus), 122 (bottom-Paul Readman), 126 (top-mika makkonen), 126 (bottom-David Freund), 127 (top-Elvira Schaefer), 127 (bottom-Ivano Police), 131 (Mary Lane), 138 (David Freund), 139 (top right-Katherine Garrenson), 140 (top-David Foltz), 141 (bottom-Katherine Garrenson), 145 (Jim Lundgren), 148 (Eric Forehand), 156 (Don Faucher), 164 (Christine Rondeau)

Image from the American Philosophical Society: 159 (bottom)

Images Copyright © Railway Station Productions, LLC: 160 (top), 161

INDEX